MODERN VIEWS

INSPIRED BY THE

MIES VAN DER ROHE

FARNSWORTH HOUSE

AND THE

PHILIP JOHNSON

GLASS HOUSE

601 West 26th Street, 18th floor
New York, NY 10001 USA
Tel.: 212 989-6810 Fax: 212 647-0005
www.assouline.com
ISBN: 9782759404674
Design by Camille Dubois
Color separation: Luc A.C. Retouching
Printed in China.

MODERN VIEWS

INSPIRED BY THE

MIES VAN DER ROHE

FARNSWORTH HOUSE

AND THE

PHILIP JOHNSON

GLASS HOUSE

ASSOULINE

TABLE OF CONTENTS

A Message from the National Trust for Historic Preservation

David J. Brown, Acting President, National Trust for Historic Preservation

As two of the most recent additions to our national network of historic sites, Farnsworth House and the Philip Johnson Glass House provide the National Trust for Historic Preservation with a powerful argument for the importance of protecting twentieth-century design.

These two iconic places—among our nation's greatest architectural and cultural assets—embody the essential place Modernism must have in the preservation movement of the twenty-first century.

Their partnership through MODERN VIEWS is an important part of our broader Modernism + Recent Past program, which is dedicated to scholarship, fostering dialogue, and devising best practices for the preservation of architecture from the period. As we reach out to people working in communities nationwide to save the Modern landmarks that matter to them, we are bolstered by our experiences in maintaining and promoting these two irreplaceable masterworks.

That two sites could inspire so much creativity and support as chronicled in *Modern Views* illustrates just how vital these sites are, not merely as a reflection of our architectural past but as a source of inspiration for the future. If you have not already visited Farnsworth House or the Glass House, I invite you to experience them for yourself. I know you will come away committed to the need to save our nation's threatened twentieth-century landmarks. In the meantime, I know you will find your own inspiration through *Modern Views*.

Directors' Note

Whitney French, Executive Director, Farnsworth House
Christy MacLear, Executive Director, Philip Johnson Glass House

Two architects: Ludwig Mies van der Rohe and Philip Johnson. Two clients: one a Midwestern doctor, the other the architect himself. Two sites: an Illinois plain and a rolling Connecticut estate. One idea: a house made of glass.

The silent dialogue between the Mies van der Rohe Farnsworth House (1945–51) and the Philip Johnson Glass House (1949) is long and complex, and the two structures' ideals and effects have intrigued students of art, architecture, and design for decades. As *Modern Views* proves, this conversation is ongoing and relevant.

It is also not limited to the design professions: We witness the same discussions on every tour, every year. The MODERN VIEWS project attempts to extend the conversation, by offering the ninety-five participants an opportunity to share how these two Modernist icons have influenced their thoughts and practice, and to do so across multiple platforms—the book, exhibitions, and an auction to support our mutual preservation projects.

As executive directors of the Farnsworth House and the Glass House, we, too, are inspired daily by these houses. We are honored to help ensure that they are available for access to an international list of admirers, and we are proud to present this collection of ideas, critiques, remembrances, and visuals. This book is a modest attempt to capture a broad dialogue that has endured for more than sixty years, and will continue to do so for generations. We are eternally grateful for your support.

FOREWORD

Paul Goldberger

The building as muse: That is the idea behind *Modern Views*, for which nearly one hundred distinguished architects, artists, designers, and landscape architects have created works that are in some way inspired by either Farnsworth House, Ludwig Mies van der Rohe's extraordinary masterpiece in Plano, Illinois, or the Glass House, the centerpiece of Philip Johnson's estate in New Canaan, Connecticut—or both. That these two sublime buildings can both excite and challenge designers is no surprise; they have been doing so for more than half a century, and in a sense, the ninety-five artworks featured here are an attempt to give concrete form to the great influence that these two works of architecture have had on the design sensibility of our time.

What may be even more remarkable than their impact on artists, architects, and designers, however, is the effect that both buildings have come to have on everyone else—the broader culture at large. Neither house, of course, was unknown, and both are among the most photographed pieces of architecture of the twentieth century. But relatively few people had seen them until the early twenty-first century, when Farnsworth House became a property of the National Trust for Historic Preservation, and when the Glass House (willed to the Trust by Philip Johnson in 1986) opened to the public. The Farnsworth House, in particular, was known mainly through photographs, even to many architectural cognoscenti, since its site in the Chicago exurbs is relatively inconvenient and the house remained in private hands until just a few years ago, when it was purchased by the Trust at auction, in a bold gesture that underscored the Trust's commitment to the importance of saving Modernist architecture.

Philip Johnson, who lived at the Glass House until his death at the age of ninety-eight in 2005, at least gave a lot of large parties, and he tended to welcome visitors. But even Johnson at his most sociable did not open the door as wide as the National Trust has been able to do, making it possible for anyone to experience this glass box set in the midst of a forty-seven-acre landscape.

Together, these two National Trust sites make the point that the cool, austere, glass-and-steel Modernism of the International Style—a style that Johnson, in his 1932 book, *The International Style*, written with Henry-Russell Hitchcock, gave a name to—is not just the province of large, impersonal office buildings but a way of making architecture that can be delicate, intimate, and subtle. As this period of Modernism becomes more and more a part of history, the presence of these two buildings as public places will, I think, have a major impact on the way in which Modern architecture is viewed in the United States. While a handful of other International Style houses have been preserved as historic sites before, none are as important to the history of twentieth-century architecture as Farnsworth House and the Glass House, and until now none has been under the stewardship of the National Trust, itself a kind of imprimatur. (Indeed, the fact that both the Farnsworth and the Glass House are National Trust sites, just like the Gothic Revival mansion Lyndhurst and the Jeffersonian plantation Belle Grove, might be said to confirm the degree to which International Style modernism is no longer the radical idea it once was.)

It is particularly gratifying that the two houses are able to be visited for another reason, which is that only by seeing both can you understand how different they are from each other. Some of the architects take note of this in the statements that accompany their drawings (others, curiously, do not). When you have seen them both, as anyone now can do, you cannot ever think of them as anything but distant architectural cousins, each determined to stand for a set of ideas that are its own, however much there may still be a faint family resemblance.

The Glass House, which was finished first, in 1949, was designed after Farnsworth House, and Philip Johnson's debt to Mies van der Rohe is incalculable. But Johnson broke away from Mies even as he paid tribute to him. The Glass House sits solidly on the earth, foursquare, a classical temple rendered in glass and black-painted steel and set on a brick podium, and is the centerpiece of a large estate that contains numerous other buildings, each of which represents a phase of Johnson's eclectic career. The Farnsworth House is a thing unto itself, its white steel-and-glass form hovering magically and delicately above the earth. The Glass House is full of drama and is in every way a splendid showpiece. The Farnsworth House is quieter, and deeper. It is gentle, and there seems at first to be almost nothing to it—a house so light it might float away. But as with a Zen garden, Mies's perfect spareness forces us inward, and confers upon us the awesome power of the sublime.

The Farnsworth House under construction, 1950.

Preparing a travertine slab for installation at Farnsworth House, 1950.

The Farnsworth House site after a Fox River flood, 1950.

PHYLLIS LAMBERT REFLECTS

Phyllis Lambert (b. 1927) is an eminent architect, preservationist, lecturer, and curator, as well as the founding director and chair of the board of trustees for the Canadian Centre for Architecture in Montreal, the leading international research center and museum for architecture. The following reflections are from an interview conducted by Dorothy Dunn of the Glass House Oral History Project on April 9, 2010, at the Canadian Centre for Architecture.

Phyllis Lambert on the Glass House and Farnsworth House

Philip's place is a narrative. Mies's place is not a narrative. It is a place of contemplation, like a Rothko. Mies told me, "You never know how colorful nature is until you're in a glass house."

Mies's building is a single object in a landscape. It was a great breakthrough in architecture. It was his first clear-span building. It's the first really clear-structured building. He worked very slowly, very carefully to understand, as he would say, how to put two pieces of steel together—this structure that holds up the roof and the floor plane. It was the clear-span idea. After that came Crown Hall and then the great building in Berlin. Creating Farnsworth House was a real breakthrough. For Mies, it was a structural issue. He said, "We do structural architecture."

For Philip, the Glass House wasn't a structural issue. It was a romantic idea—a glass house.

Philip had all sorts of ideas that you see in his drawings. He was going all over the place. His first idea wasn't to make a glass house at all.

The Glass House was a complex with the Brick House. Each building at the Glass House follows Philip's trajectory, from Modernism to postmodernism. It was a wonderful place for him to experiment.

It's a wonderful place to be in. Philip used to talk about his great wallpaper, because it changed all the time. But architecturally, compared to Farnsworth House, it's just a toy.

I was at the Glass House often and in different circumstances. I knew the Glass House very early. I remember sitting there with [Eero] Saarinen and Philip and Aline, Saarinen's wife, talking about who should be the architect [for the Seagram Building]. It was before Mies was chosen.

It was just so fantastic, going to bed in the guest room, turning the dimmer down. Lying in that pink room was like being in the desert with the sand. It was gorgeous. The leather in Philip's bathroom . . . It smelled so good!

I visited once in the early fall. Philip decided to light the fire, but he forgot to remove the chimney cover. He said that we had to go up on the roof to take the cover off. I got stuck up there. I was terrified to come down!

Philip was very interested in history. He was always exploring historic ideas and precedents. Most architects never talk about their precedents. Mies certainly never did . . . [Actually,] yes, he did. He talked about [Karl Friedrich] Schinkel. Philip did too, but very differently. Standing on the platform of Farnsworth House, that platform is pure Schinkel.

Philip was influenced by the views in Schinkel's paintings and prints—looking down the valley and into a rich view of woodland valley or hills. Of course, Schinkel's views are of Europe. In Connecticut, Philip started cutting trees down to make vistas. Then he finally put that little object down in the pond. It was fun when he did that.

Mies and Philip had very different attitudes toward the landscape. Farnsworth is a work of art, a great work of art, just set down in the

Philip Johnson, Mies van der Rohe, and Phyllis Lambert, during a 1955 meeting on the Seagram Building in New York, pictured behind.

landscape. The Glass House is a construct. At Farnsworth, the landscape is immediate. You're there. You're in it. The tree, the field, the river is right there. It's not something you see from afar. It's around you.

Mies placed his house right in front of one big tree. [Mimicking his German accent] "Vun big tree." This was always his idea. Wonderful. He sited it himself, staking out exactly where the house would be and the columns.

Philip distanced the landscape. He put his house on a precipice where you look at the landscape, way down there. It's very picturesque.

The Glass House is a romantic idea. Light allowed Philip to break with Mies and what he had termed the International Style.

Philip told me this: When Mies first came to see the Glass House, Philip had lights all over the place. Mies said, "It looks like a hot dog stand." Philip then asked "that great genius Richard Kelly" what to do. He said, with one bulb in the house, you have six bulbs. One bulb is reflected in all the glass. Kelly had gone to Yale to study architecture. He was interested in lighting, and he knew that the new glass architecture had to be dealt with differently. He became involved with the theater school at Yale and picked up lighting skills there and developed a theory. Philip took this over—the dramatic concept of washing walls with light [by intensely lighting the lawn at the edge of the Glass House], creating areas of interest through light and sparkle [by lighting the trees].

Philip treated his property as an estate. He didn't do just a Glass House. He did a brick house and a glass house. People always forget that.

[The] Seagram Building isn't just a building. It's a building and a plaza.

Phyllis Lambert on the Seagram Building

Lambert was instrumental in bringing Ludwig Mies van der Rohe to the project initiated by her father, Samuel Bronfman, C.E.O. of Seagram, in 1954, to build a new corporate headquarters in New York for the company's centenary. She was henceforth named director of planning of the Seagram Building (1954–58). In 1984, the Seagram Building was awarded the Twenty-Five Year Award for an architectural project of enduring significance by the American Institute of Architects.

When did I first become aware of Mies? I was living in Paris. I knew that my father was interested in building a building in New York to celebrate the hundred-year anniversary of the Seagram Corporation. I saw an image of a proposed building. That's when I wrote my famous "No, no, no!" letter. I must say, it's an amazing letter. I wrote about the Renaissance, which he misunderstood. I wrote about the microcosm and the macrocosm. I described the new glass buildings in New York—the Lever House and the United Nations building. They're heavy, but they look light. And then I said, Well, what should a building be today?

My father said to come back and choose the marble. I said I would do no such thing. My mother said, "Well, let's see what she can do." So I came back. I started learning very fast.

I was born the day I started working on the Seagram Building. I date my birth from then.

I met Philip Johnson because a friend of mine, Marie Alexander, worked with Alfred Barr at the Museum of Modern Art. Alfred said, "Well, go and see Philip, but remember he's leaving the museum. He's doing his own work." Of course, Philip was very excited about the idea that one could build a great building.

Eero Saarinen was the one who clarified the issue of how to think about architects, creating the categories of "those architects who could and shouldn't, those who should and couldn't, and those who should and could." It was pure Eero, the list maker. Everyone was talking about it, but Saarinen gave the process a structure, and that's why one remembers it. The things that don't have structure you don't remember.

Everyone gives Philip the credit for taking me around everywhere, but that is sheer nonsense. I talked to critics. I went to see all the architects in their offices. I traveled to Boston, Cincinnati, and Detroit. I went to see [Minoru] Yamasaki, [Walter] Gropius, [Louis] Kahn, [Eero] Saarinen. Everybody was talking about Mies. "I would do this differently from Mies. I do that differently from Mies. I would have more sculptural forms than Mies." It was quite interesting as I think of it now. We eliminated [Gordon] Bunshaft right away. He'd done the Lever House, but I thought, Well, why not get the master?

I went to Chicago to meet Mies. We had lunch at the Pearson Hotel because he lived right next door. I asked him the same questions I asked everybody else: "Who do you think should build the building?" I never asked anybody if they wanted to build the building. That would be sort of ridiculous. So I asked him who he thought should do it.

I asked him about Le Corbusier. I was really interested in Le Corbusier. Everybody else had told me, "Oh, Le Corbusier, being from France, he wouldn't know the materials, rules, engineers." Nobody was very generous. But Mies was so generous. He said, "He's a great architect, and it doesn't make any difference if he has worked here or not."

I liked the attitude of the man. There was nothing petty. There was something so grand about him. And then, of course, I saw this extraordinary building, 860 Lake Shore Drive. Have you ever seen it? It's amazing, especially then. This was 1954.

My father had asked Lou Crandall, head of the Fuller Company, to build the building as if it were his own. He agreed on my choice of Mies, and Mies came to New York to have luncheon with my mother, my father, Philip, and me. Lou Crandall asked me what would happen if Mies, who was seventy-two, died. I said that I didn't know his office. I'd been there, but I didn't know the capacities of people there. So Crandall said, "What do you think about Philip?" I thought that was a great idea, and so I asked Mies what he thought. Mies said to Philip, "*Ja*, shall we make it van der Rohe and Johnson?"

No question about it, Mies was the master. Philip knew that and interested himself in the industrial design issues. He was interested in new handles for the doors, new taps for the bathrooms, new valves, the graphics—all kinds of designed things. And then, of course, he finally did the lighting for the building and the Four Seasons. Those were both huge contributions.

My role was to make the building that Mies wanted to make. I wanted to make sure that happened. I just pushed everything out of the way that got in the way.

Phyllis Lambert on MODERN VIEWS

MODERN VIEWS is inspired by the dialogue between Farnsworth House and the Glass House—between Ludwig Mies van der Rohe and Philip Johnson.
The project invites great minds in contemporary art, architecture, and design to continue that dialogue through submissions of work and statements.

The Glass House and Farnsworth House are two great manifestations of Modernism in the United States. There's no question about that. And they were built around the same time.

In both places, you can explore the themes: excess, or lack of excess; sense of place; sense of landscape; a place of contemplation; modernism; classicism. During tours, you can ask where and when these ideas existed before. Visitors can talk about where and when they have experienced these qualities and ideas—in the past, present, and how they think they are relevant to the future. Visitors can define their own context for what they are looking at and experiencing.

Inviting students to these sites is, above all, most important. They should visit with someone who can introduce one or two important questions. Each generation has different interests, and you have to work with that. You have to reflect on what people are interested in. Ten to thirteen people on a tour is all right, but twenty would be too many.

Of course, preserving the authenticity of both places is important. The approaches to both houses and the landscapes must be properly treated. It's important that the houses are properly furnished and with proper materials.

Philip had a great sense of materials. Mies loved his building in

Washington, D.C.—Dumbarton Oaks—because he thought the materials were so fine.

Philip was a wonderful writer. And the way he talked . . . I'm envious. He had a fantastic memory. He spoke German. He spoke Greek. He was fascinating. I loved the way he expressed ideas sharply.

Mies would express ideas very differently. He designed a theater in Mannheim. It was big and was never built, but it had a concrete seating shell. He said that the seating shell came out of the concrete the way a hand comes out of the wrist. It was very physical.

Like all architecture, you have to be in the Glass House and be in Farnsworth House to understand them. People forget that architecture is visceral. Everything has to come together—your mind and your gut, the back of your head, your shoulders, everything.

Recorded for the Glass House Oral History Project by Edgardo Resto of R.B.H. Multimedia.
Transcript edited by Dorothy Dunn.

Dr. Edith Farnsworth and one of her poodles
during the construction of the house, 1950.

WHAT'S IN A NAME:
That Which We Call a Glass House

Sylvia Lavin

Alone, her back to the house, Edith Farnsworth seems to be looking for any sign of life in this grim and desolate late-winter landscape. Only the dog is happy, happy to be running away from the house in which, with hindsight, we know paw prints were never really at home. The house is not yet finished, nothing but an empty cage of steel, and yet it still seems full of Edith Farnsworth's fear of being caught on the inside, imprisoned in this, the world's supposedly most open house, the house with the freest of all possible free plans.

Everyone is happy, happy to be celebrating a wedding day at the New Canaan estate. Images of the good life overtake everyone, even the photographer. The only reason for us to intrude now on the privacy of this long-ago event is that the festivities took place in the shadow of the Glass House. The house is so confident in its persistence and presence that it doesn't even need to be seen. It's enough to observe, in another snapshot, Philip Johnson against a landscape with a rock wall to know that the Glass House lurks nearby.

No two photographs could better play out the agonizing comparisons that Farnsworth House and Glass House have always solicited. From birth, as it were, the two have been like Siamese twins, joined at the hip in a relationship of mutual attraction and simultaneous horror. They seem to have so much in common—they are both rectangular one-room pavilions, held up by steel, wrapped in glass, and surrounded by Edenic landscapes. How could they not be the best of architectural friends? Yet they seem to give different answers to virtually every question one could pose: To be on the ground or not to be on the ground? To be brown or to be white? To place your beam under the roof prosaically or to place your beam outside the roof and floor to suspend the whole in virtual midair?

Worst of all, these close and intimate friends have so much to fight over and envy in how they are seen by others: the elder master's masterpiece, the student upstart's crowning achievement; the original from the era of the Modernist cult of originality, the copy from the era of the postmodernist cult of appropriation. Placing them side by side is like comparing a human being with a gorilla and leads to just as much astonishment that sharing 98 percent of their DNA can yield such unfathomable difference.

Houses, the homes of life, themselves have many lives, lives linked but not reducible to daily wear and tear, domestic arrangements, and other private matters. Houses indeed stage and frame life within them, but they themselves also live in the outside world and are framed by the world's perception of them. For example, some are given names not so much by the owners and architects but by history. Only history, with its unmatched flair for irony, could have determined that Farnsworth House would forever bear the name of a woman who barely lived there, faced the architect in court, and felt effaced by him and his minimalism. Who would have guessed that the name "Glass House," the culmination of one hundred years of effort and

The wedding of Rosamond Bernier and John Russell, at Philip Johnson's estate, 1975.

research, would be awarded to Johnson the gadfly and godfather and not to Mies the master? After all, Mies's early skyscrapers are often referred to as "glass towers." For some observers, a more proper name for the Johnson house would be "After Mies" or "Mies by Johnson," like a precocious work of postmodern appropriation.

Even though the name of Farnsworth House identifies its commissioning client, the appellation seems scant compensation for the more profound forms of erasure the house effected on her possessions, her title, and her desire to be there. (Shortly after the house was completed, Dr. Farnsworth and Mies ended up in a famous court battle: Mies sued Farnsworth; she countersued.) No accident or matter of personal misunderstanding, Edith Farnsworth's public distance from the house was a necessary if collateral effect of Mies's intent to yoke the house to historical rather than personal forces and to propel its architecture toward the nameless timelessness of utopia.

As a title, "the Glass House" is utterly impersonal, a perhaps exaggerated but still clinical designation of the building's material. The name furthermore is generous and gives the house a perfect grade in the pursuit for medium specificity and material purity, the formal ideals of the time established by the art critic Clement Greenberg—after all, it's not called "the Glass, Brick, and Steel House."

The name is thus both idealizing and abstract, and the words still conjure up the star-studded life of Philip Johnson, who hosted parties and social gatherings of legend on the premises of his estate. The wedding of art lecturer Rosamond Bernier to *New York Times* art critic John Russell, observed above, was not a rare occasion. In fact, the house was frequently under the lights, used as a TV studio, and was the subject of countless portraits and shoots. Someone or something important was always being photographed at the Glass House, and if they weren't famous when they arrived they were closer to celebrity when they left.

And though Edith Farnsworth was famously anxious about where to put her garbage and fearful that the closet doors—really just suspended panels behind which she had to cower while changing clothes—might compromise her modesty, the inhabitants of and visitors to the Glass House felt aggrandized and propelled to perform, as if under a magical spotlight and perpetual camera. The normally demure Andy Warhol, for example (demure in that he was generally more interested in filming others and surrounding himself with stars and stars in the making), bypassed the normal attraction to and

The Glass House, circa 1949.

1. ARCHITECTS

Johnston Marklee

Sharon Johnston and Mark Lee Johnston Marklee ▲

Architectural conventions evolve until confronted by masterpieces. Usually born of necessity rather than caprice, these masterpieces transcend construction, enabling one to fully grasp the cultural changes of the zeitgeist. Among Modernist conventions, the evolution of the window has one of the longest historical lineages. Whether serving as a device for framing, an interface between interior and exterior, or as a medium between domestic space and spectacle, the window perpetuated theoretical inquiries reflective of its epoch. The evolution of the window came to an end in the Glass House and Farnsworth House. Developments which came after these masterpieces are but variations or perpetual reiterations of what has come before.

Daniel Libeskind Studio Daniel Libeskind

At my 1987 *City Edge* project in Berlin (Flottwellstrasse 24), a photograph of Mies looks down along an oblique red line propped up by structural supports. His gaze is supported by Philip Johnson's book on Mies, and is attached by four screws to the base.The base is a white field upon which are traced, in reverse, handwritten verses of modern thought. In a mirror, these words become almost legible. The traces contain transferred fragments of thought: Mondrian, Celan, Nietzsche, and Heidegger. From a distance they resemble a piece of earth plowed by previous generations, now covered by snow.

Rafael Viñoly **Rafael Viñoly Architects**

Less is More or More or Less

This is the story of an idea and its transfiguration through the inevitable mill of its consumption. While one needs no words to be described (its magic is in its integrity), the other requires a text to explain its legitimacy. These two houses are the story of the power of art and the power of money. Two equal partners in the creation

Brigitte Shim and Howard Sutcliffe

Shim-Sutcliffe Architects

The undulating glass wall of our Integral House has a different relationship to nature than either the Mies van der Rohe Farnsworth House or the Philip Johnson Glass House. Unlike the still-picture quality of nature viewed through the plate glass windows, this wall of syncopated solid voids creates a cinematic relationship to the forest that is always changing—weaving architecture and nature together through movement. As a result, the view from within has changed from gaze to dream as one moves through the space.

Dirk Denison Dirk Denison Architects

Modernism's embrace of technological advancement changed our lifestyle, such that our activities began to collage spatially. Disparate rooms no longer suited the fluidity of modern life. Large panes of glass allowed walls to fade away to frames, providing views out and in. Nature was embraced, enjoyed, and abstracted. The Glass House and Farnsworth House exemplify these tendencies, and my Cohodes House multiplies their effects. With these houses opening internally, layered and framed views of nature are projected back upon the architecture, creating a folded intimacy rather than a binary vista. A base 4 (family of four) is crossed with a base 2 (self and other) to establish the spatial organization. Each space is its own object, registering along the matrix, yet none are distinctly experienced. Diagonal lines fold the space, breaking open the envelope. Sunlight pierces through.

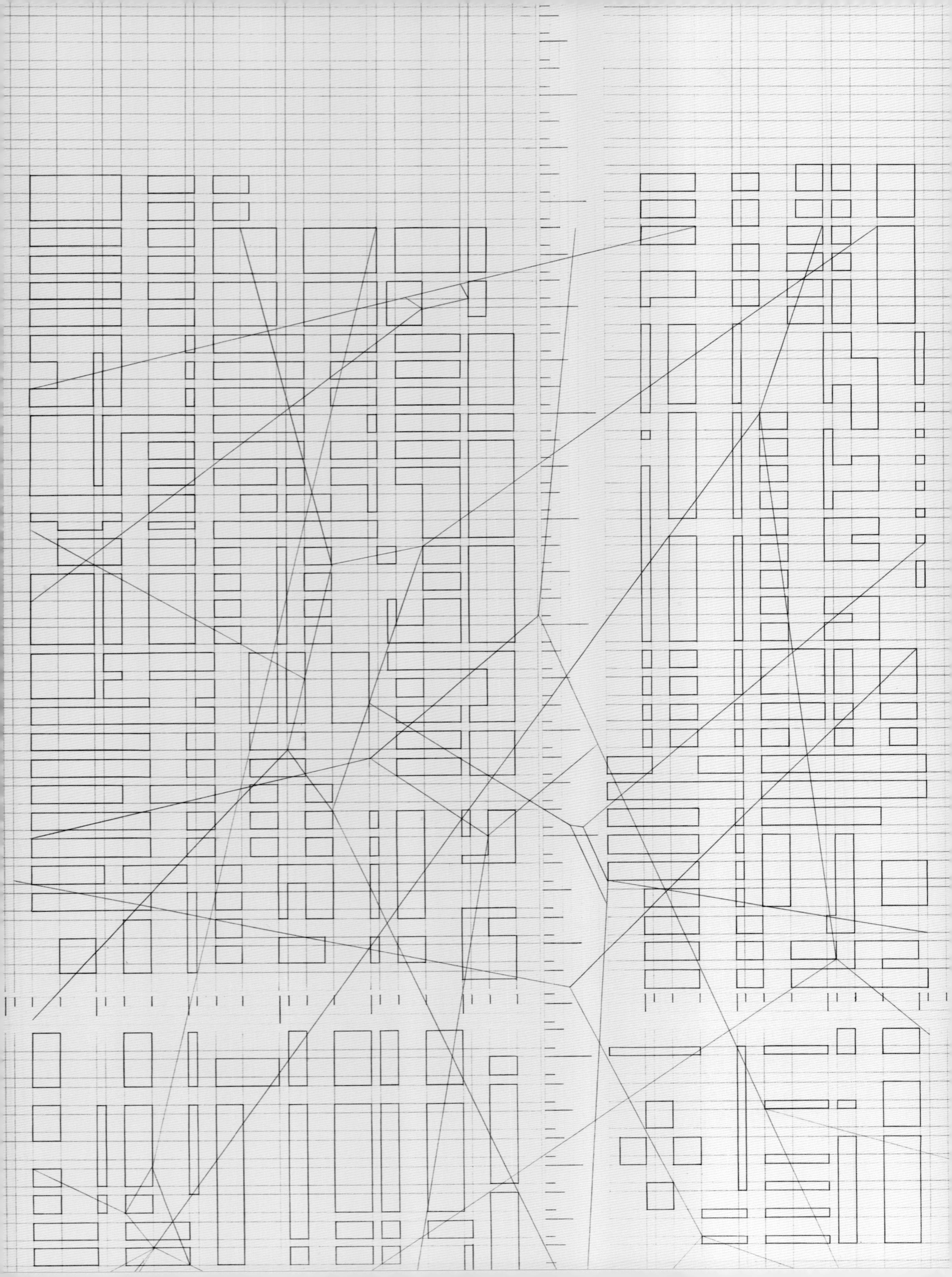

Thomas Beeby **Hammond Beeby Rupert Ainge Architects**

The Glass House: Search for Precedent

Mies sketched a house near Potsdam for himself in 1913. If we assume from the drawing that he intended a double-square central salon, this mirrored, Corinthian room would be composed in the Franco-Prussian tradition. The walls would be divided into base, pilaster, and entablature zones. The plan would be divided by a grid into an odd number of bays in both directions. Pilasters would be centered on grid lines, and all openings (alternating with mirrors) would be centered between grid lines. The corner detail would be reflected symmetrically 90 degrees with no distortion of architectural elements. The house was never realized, but classical dreams lived on.

72
8
4
2
8
24
72

Hans Hollein Atelier Hollein

I have seen Farnsworth House in reality, experienced several times the Glass House, met the architects—Mies van der Rohe during the time of my graduate studies at the Illinois Institute of Technology in Chicago and Philip Johnson many times in New York, New Canaan, and elsewhere—had multiple encounters with the Robie House, as well as a personal encounter with Frank Lloyd Wright at Taliesin shortly before his death—all in the late fifties.

These encounters were seminal for me. I understood the potential and radiation of those buildings as architectural manifestos and signals into the future of architecture. *Extension*—into space—and *Reduction*.

I was part of this future and made my own architectural statements based partly on those two glass boxes but also on free sculptural shapes cantilevering into space. Building up and digging down. And I thought about more minimal dwellings—telephone booths, space capsules—and further into nonphysical environments: an architecture of the pill.

Pavilion by Hans Hollein
top of Rothschild Castle 2007

Hans Hollein
2010

Farmsworth House
24/12/2009

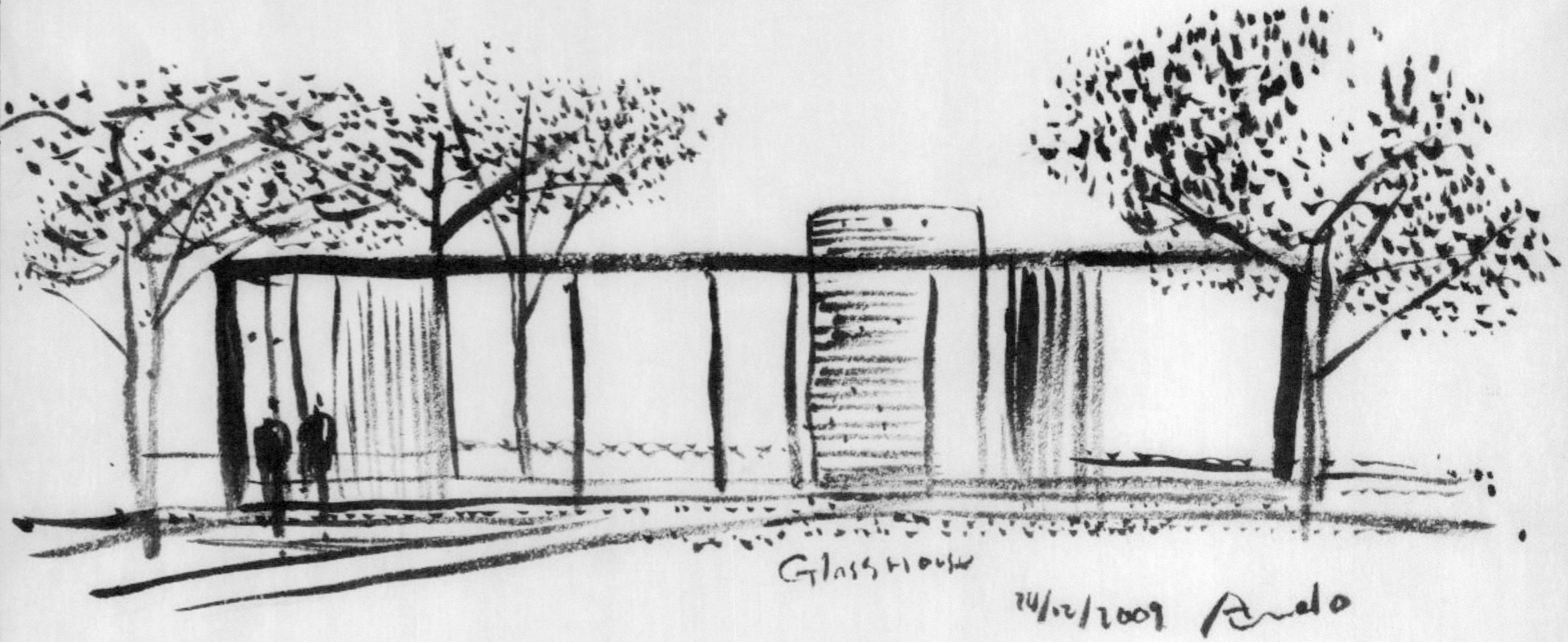

Tadao Ando Tadao Ando Architect & Associates

Two Sides of Modernism

Mies van der Rohe's Farnsworth House is a masterpiece of architecture that symbolizes twentieth-century Modernism. It is a quiet architecture with a transparent logic that penetrates down to the details and materials. With intuition and perfectionism, Mies silently achieved in Farnsworth House a culmination of the most beautiful and magnificent architectural theorem. Philip Johnson verified that theorem with a vast vocabulary. Therefore, his Glass House represents Modern architecture criticism. Mies and Johnson complemented Modern architecture mutually.

Hani Rashid **Asymptote Architecture**

Diller Scofidio + Renfro

The renovation of the Brasserie restaurant in the Seagram Building in 2000 reconciled the conceptual legacies of the two Modern masters behind its original design. Taking a cue from Philip Johnson's iconic interior design, the gutted shell was resurfaced with thin liners that sometimes lift away to become structural, spatial, and functional elements. While Mies van der Rohe's Seagram Building is considered to be the quintessential Modernist glass tower, the restaurant is lodged in its stone base and lacks both glass and view. This irony prompted a series of alternate responses to the relation between glass and vision.

Jeanne Gang Studio Gang Architects

I made a sketch of Farnsworth House as I remember it from a winter visit. Instead of the steel-and-glass structure that I expected, or the sophisticated framing device it was supposed to be, the house was something I had never anticipated.

John Vinci Vinci | Hamp Architects

I had never seen a graphic comparison of Edith Farnsworth's house by Ludwig Mies van der Rohe and Philip Johnson's Glass House. Elevations of Johnson's house had not appeared in any of the publications I had read. I began by drawing the elevations from existing plans and photographs, and with dimensions supplied by the Philip Johnson Glass House manager, I formulated these drawings.

In the seventeenth century, Shah Jahan, who commissioned the white marble Taj Mahal to be his wife's tomb, considered building a similar structure of black basalt for his own final resting place across the river from his wife's mausoleum. The symbolism of designating white for a female and black for a male in mausoleums has also been noted in the work of Louis Sullivan. In the 1890s, for Chicago's Graceland Cemetery, Sullivan designed a tomb in dark, polished granite for Martin Ryerson, a lumber magnate, and one in light gray limestone for Carrie Eliza Getty, the wife of Ryerson's business partner.

Similarly, Philip Johnson's house, firmly grounded in black steel, represents the masculine, and Farnsworth House, elevated above the ground and designed in white painted steel, represents the feminine.These drawings are conceived as an imagined landscape.

Léon Krier

A Brief Encounter

For my first show at the Max Protetch Gallery in 1980, I was Philip's guest at one of the regular Century Club black-tie dinners, surrounded by an assortment of New York Whites and Greys. Johnson had called me a few days earlier acrcss the Atlantic. To his "You are the best architect in the world," I replied, "It isn't that difficult, is it?" When he repeated the accolade during the dinner, judging from the faces of some of the attendees, I had the distinct feeling that the applause was not so much intended to flatter me but to scold some of those present. Indeed the ceremony was one of dethronement rather than one of empowerment. Philip also said that he had no problems embracing my entire agenda. "Streets, squares, quarters"—no problem. "Classical architecture, vernacular building"—no problem at all. Even though it was never said, I am sure that it was Philip who had Arthur Drexler organize the 1985 Bofill-Krier exhibition at the Museum of Modern Art and acquire all the drawings of my Washington, D.C., master plan.

It was around that time that Philip invited me to lunch at the Four Seasons with Peter Eisenman. Philip asked outright, "Léon, how much do you need?" When he saw I didn't understand his question, he insisted, "How much money? You need money, don't you?" When I replied that I had no problems in that area, he seemed instantly to lose interest in me. We only met once more, when he showed Demetri Porphyrios and me through his New Canaan property. By that time he had gone on to deconstruction, and all electricity had vanished out of a brief relationship.

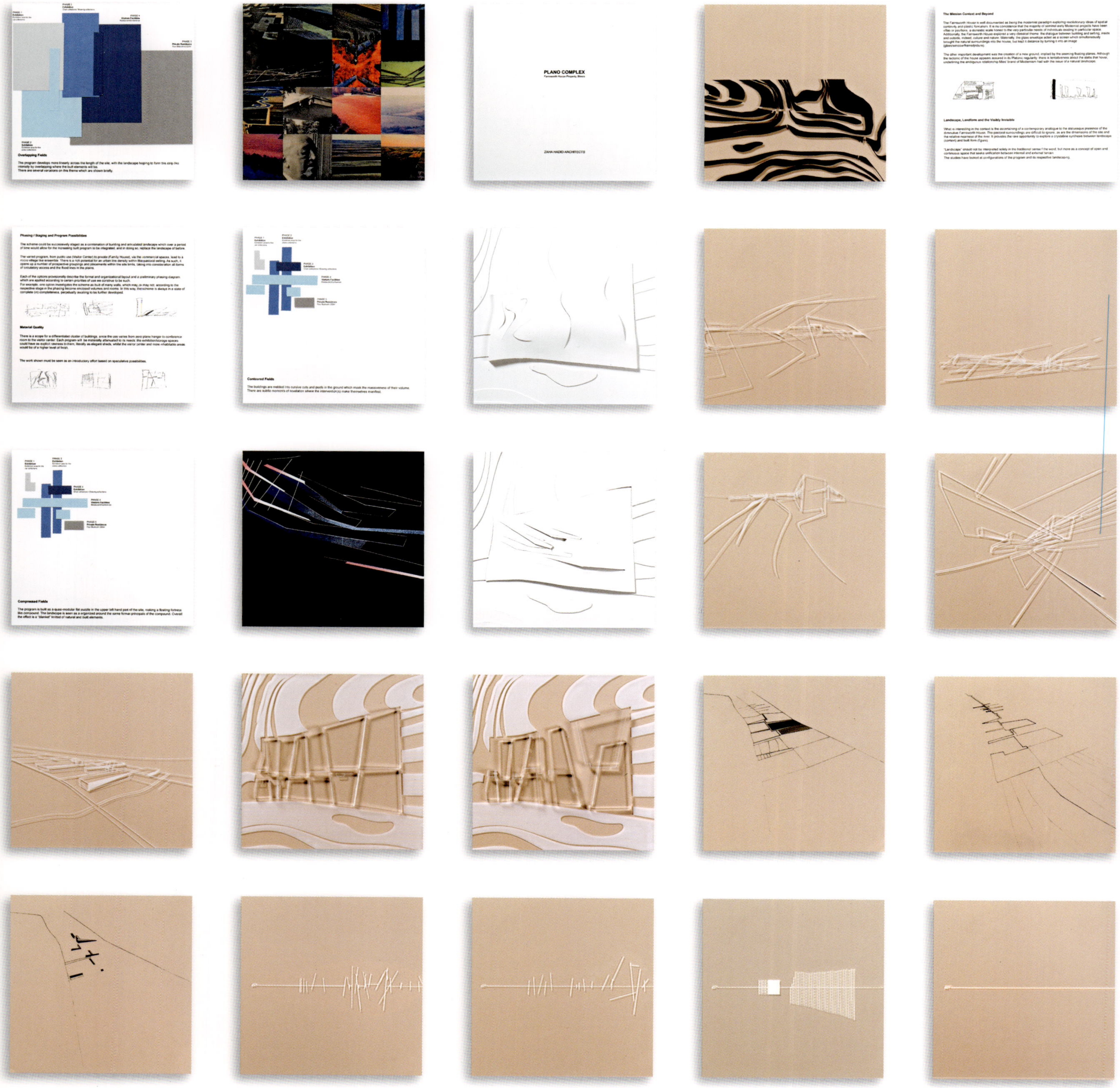
Overlapping Fields
PLANO COMPLEX
ZAHA HADID ARCHITECTS
Phasing / Staging and Program Possibilities

Zaha Hadid Zaha Hadid Architects

Ludwig Mies van der Rohe's Farnsworth House is a seminal icon and manifesto of postwar modernism. It is a fantastic effort in the dematerialization of architecture and a radical proposal of living within a natural landscape.

Ronald A. Krueck **Krueck & Sexton Architects**

We dream of living in a glass house...

"No one knows what it's like living in a glass house," Edith Farnsworth yelled at me. I was a student walking down the Fox River, and her dog barked, giving away my presence. Her anger startled me and I thought, "Why did she build one?" She lived not only in a glass house but a glass house that would become an icon of twentieth-century architecture. Its ability to function as a house would continue to go unquestioned...until the dream was *shattered* by Edith's outburst that day.

Yet the strength of this great piece of architecture survives. It will continue to be visited as a temple, just like the Greek temples of the Acropolis, which were never meant to function other than as homes for the gods.

Now Farnsworth House has evolved to its real home: a temple for all of us to visit and to dream in....

WHAT IT'S LIKE LIVING IN A GLASS HOUSE,
HAVING EYES LOOK BACK AT YOU." EDITH FARNSWORTH YELLED

Gwathmey Siegel + Associates Architects

The Glass House is an iconic Modernist example of contextual counterpoint, a man-made item set in nature, as well as a design vocabulary involving frame and objects.

The rectangular glass-enclosed pavilion is modulated by a single, cylindrical masonry form that penetrates the roof plane. Cabinetwork, an area rug, and a minimal amount of furniture demarcate the zones of use. The pavilion is sited within a landscaped setting which provides privacy as well as an extension of views from within to the natural context.

We used the Glass House as a precedent to help communicate our ideas for the 1971 redesign of Whig Hall at Princeton University, whose interior was destroyed by fire. The campus context involved the adjacency to a twin building, Clio Hall, and their side-by-side frontage on the historic Cannon Green.

The façades of Whig Hall, which related to Clio Hall, were restored following the traditional precedents.

The free side of Whig Hall faced an outdoor space framed by contemporary buildings. It provided the opportunity to articulate the new elements as objects floating within the frame of base, end columns, and cornice.

Marianne McKenna

Kuwabara Payne McKenna Blumberg Architects

In the late 1960s, Mies van der Rohe's modern TD Tower and Banking Pavilion transformed the image of Toronto. These iconic buildings catalyzed a series of "virtual Mies" towers around the original complex to define the financial heart of the city. Forty years later, we worked on the renovation of nine floors of one of the latter towers for a prominent law firm. The design focused on reclaiming the Miesian grid, transcribing the natural and urban landscape into the interior spaces. To the south, the calm dark waters of Lake Ontario are referenced by folding art walls. To the north, the grid of Mies's black curtain wall fills the windowscape.

Laurence O. Booth **Booth Hansen**

Great buildings of the twentieth century synthesize cultural and abstract traditions. Fashions, styles, and trends lose their vitality over time. Only buildings grounded in both traditions stand the test of time. Going forward, in addition, we need to focus on building performance. Total-performance buildings are the architecture of the twenty-first century.

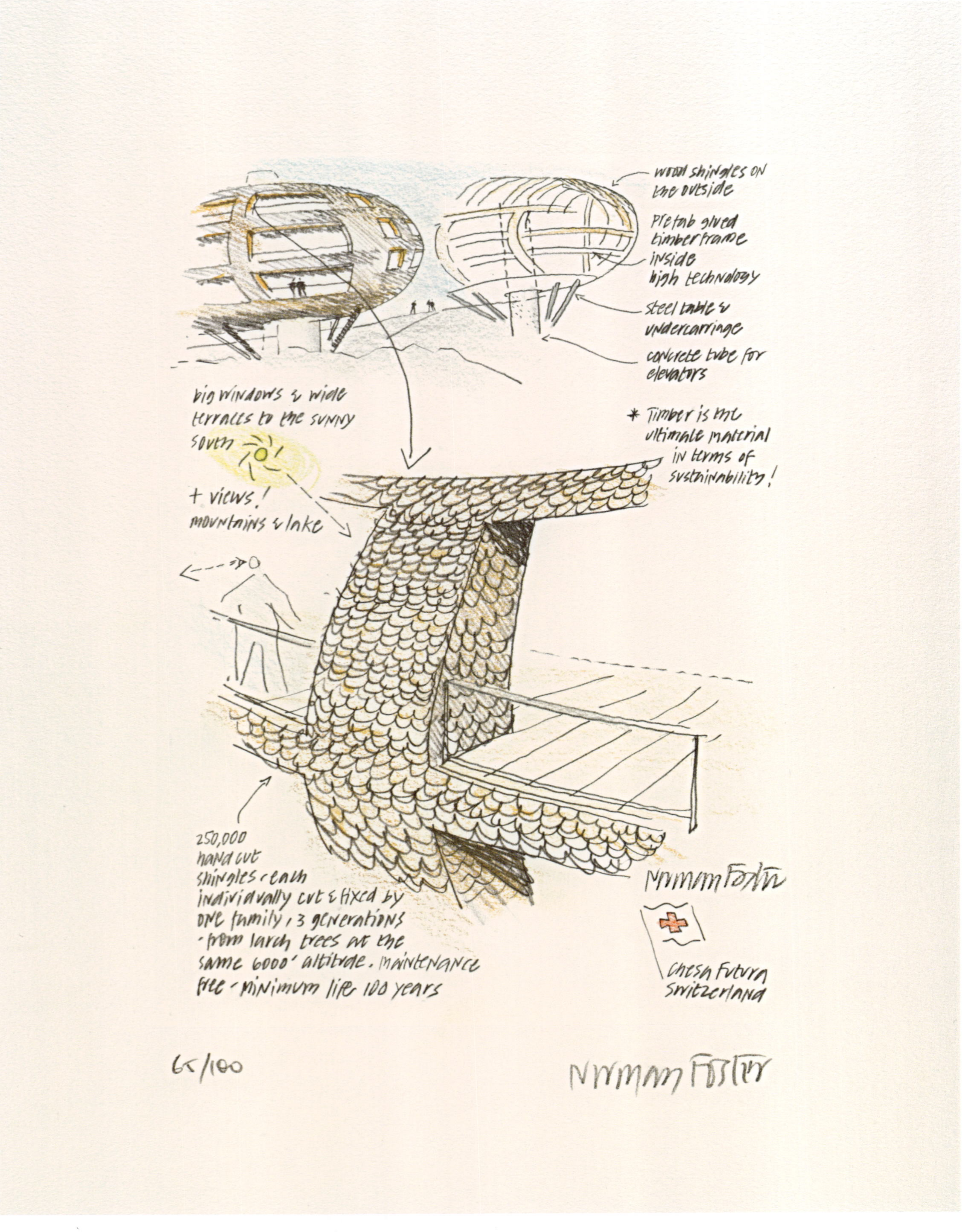

Norman Foster Foster + Partners

Toshiko Mori Toshiko Mori Architect

The Glass House is an empty vitrine of social life, encapsulated in a natural setting. The Farnsworth House is a projection of life into the infinity of space and nature. The Glass House is grounded in daily ritual (figurative) while Farnsworth House is in suspension (abstract). The proposed project is a meditation on those two opposite states regarding a "glass house." Multiple structures have specific functions and characters that pixelate and intensify each moment. Loops of time intertwine each glass pavilion. Glass pavilions are the snapshots of moments in life that unfold cinematically into a ribbon of time and space.

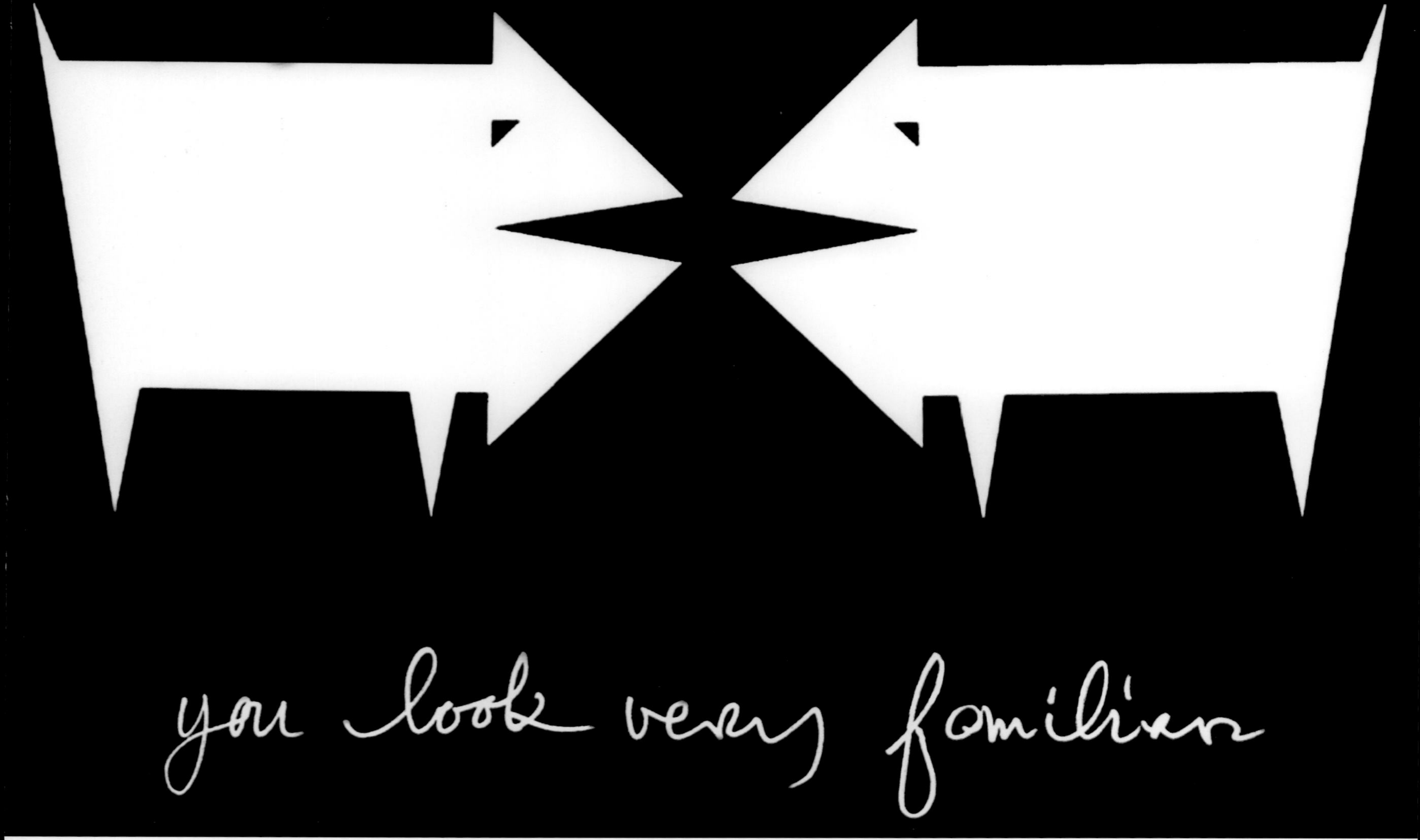

Kevin Roche **Kevin Roche John Dinkeloo and Associates**

I joined the graduate school at the Illinois Institute of Technology in the fall of 1948. The class was very small, about ten students. My impression was that the undergraduate class spent a lot of time drawing bricks, but the graduate class was much freer in activity, and Mies spent a lot of time each day with us, which was very special. He was an overwhelming—sometimes almost terrifying—presence. But it was a wonderful experience.

Late that year, word arrived that someone named Philip Johnson had built a house that copied Mies's work. I recall that this caused quite a bit of concern among Mies's disciples, although I never heard that Mies himself expressed any opinion on it at all. When Farnsworth House was completed, because visitors were not encouraged, I made a surreptitious trip to view it and was stunned by its beauty—it really was quite an epiphany.

Some years later I visited Philip's house, and while it was very impressive, very elegant, and very beautiful, in his own way Philip seemed to dominate it, and the house served as a background for him. In contrast, the extraordinary presence of Farnsworth House seemed to put Dr. Edith Farnsworth, Mies, and its tragic birth in the distant background, and the house itself remains one of the great shining moments in Modern architecture.

Thom Mayne Morphosis Architects

Johnson and Mies are inextricably linked via the Glass House. Where Mies may rightfully be credited with the idea, Johnson's decision to construct and live in a transparent house made a powerful leap to connect the intellectual to the psychological and transcendent idea of vision—a vision in which transparency operates as a useful metaphor for the psychological stance of its inhabitant. The Glass House articulates the importance of openness as intrinsic to the Modernist project. In creating and living in this transparent box, Johnson claimed this visionary notion of transparency for himself, a daily reminder of the constant oscillation between positions within and outside of one's own skin. The self becomes a project of sorts through the metaphor of skin, revealing the architect's relationship to the eyes of others, to himself, to nature and landscape. Finally it declares that, yes, the decision has been made—not simply to talk about the imperative for openness as a stance to life, but to live it.

Annabelle Selldorf Selldorf Architects

Mies van der Rohe's postulate that "form is not the goal but the result of our work" continues to be profoundly inspiring. Revisiting Farnsworth House never fails to make us confront the meaning of this statement. Indeed, Farnsworth House makes no direct reference to anything but the notion of discipline in the context of freedom. The simple, geometric forms of terrace and house floating above the pastoral landscape along the Fox River represent a radically minimal idea of structure and of domestic space, and of transforming utilitarian architecture into an exercise in proportion and detail.

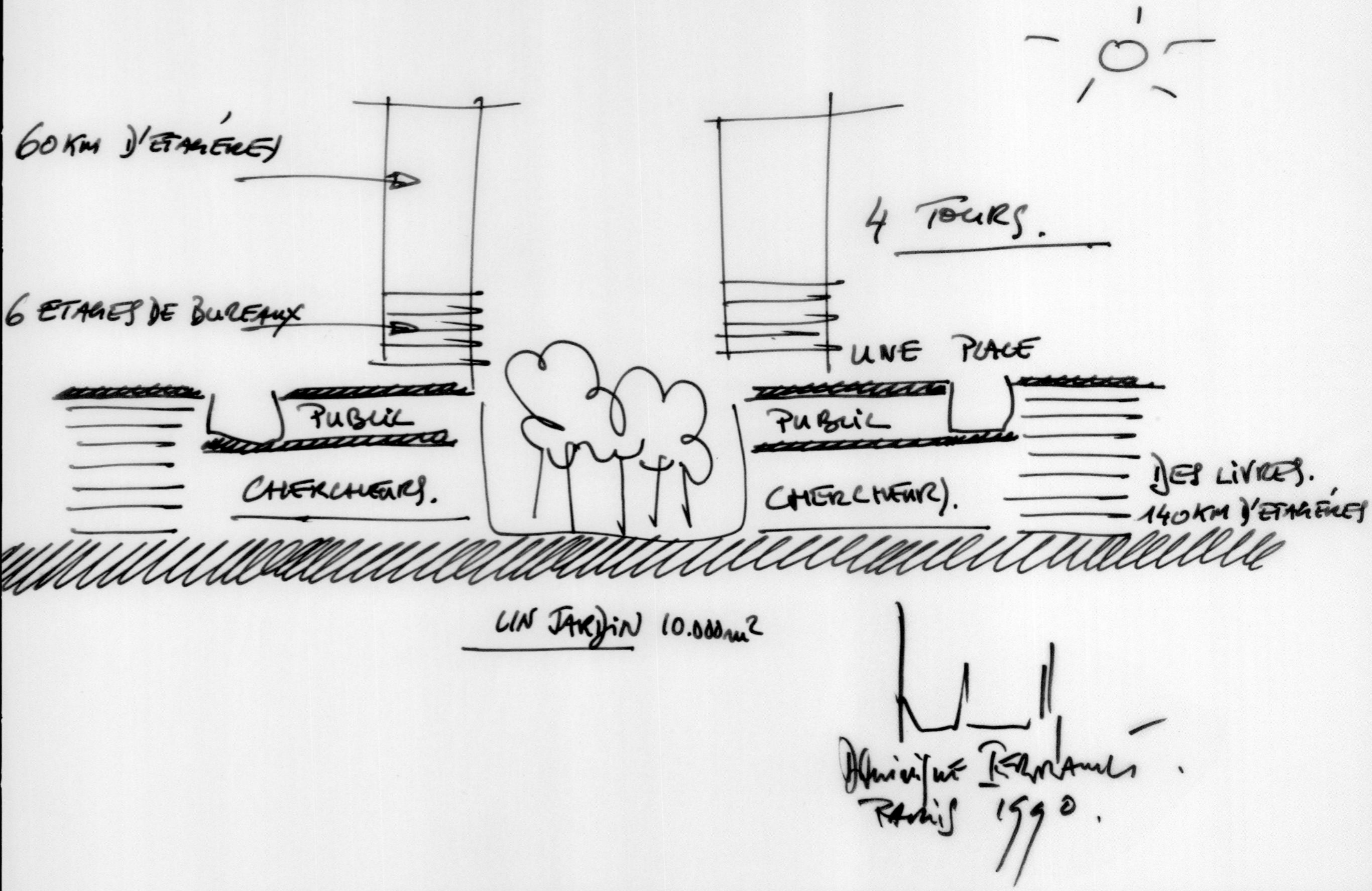

Dominique Perrault Dominique Perrault Architecture

I sincerely admire Louis Kahn and Mies van der Rohe because they share a quasi-mystical exactingness. Both men went beyond the question of humanity in their quest, and ever since my own beginnings in architecture I have oscillated between their influences. In my National Library of France project, there is a blend of their ideas, in terms of the relationship between matter and silence, which some people call neutral writing. The architecture of the National Library of France is made up of abstract concepts of emptiness and silence. They are the elements, which make it as much a library for individuals as a library of community.

Mohsen Mostafavi Dean of the Harvard Graduate School of Design

Eric Owen Moss **Eric Owen Moss Architects**

We Contemplating Us

Culture is a studied look in a fun house mirror.

The image bends and flexes.

We contemplating Us.

Sometimes crooked, rotund, or attenuated.

But never an empirical perspective.

Culture isn't evolution.

Culture isn't progress.

We gain.

We lose.

We move.

Reflections on our reflection move too.

Architecture On Defense

Architecture on defense sustains a particular moment in the mirror, and insists that moment is enduring.

Architecture *qua* architecture interrogates the culture, contests the reflected view, builds not what the view in the mirror prescribes but proscribes the view in the mirror.

Architecture *qua* architecture never ratifies the culture.

Architecture's duty today is to subvert pro forma form.

The world can always be other than it is.

New architecture can facilitate that reimagining.

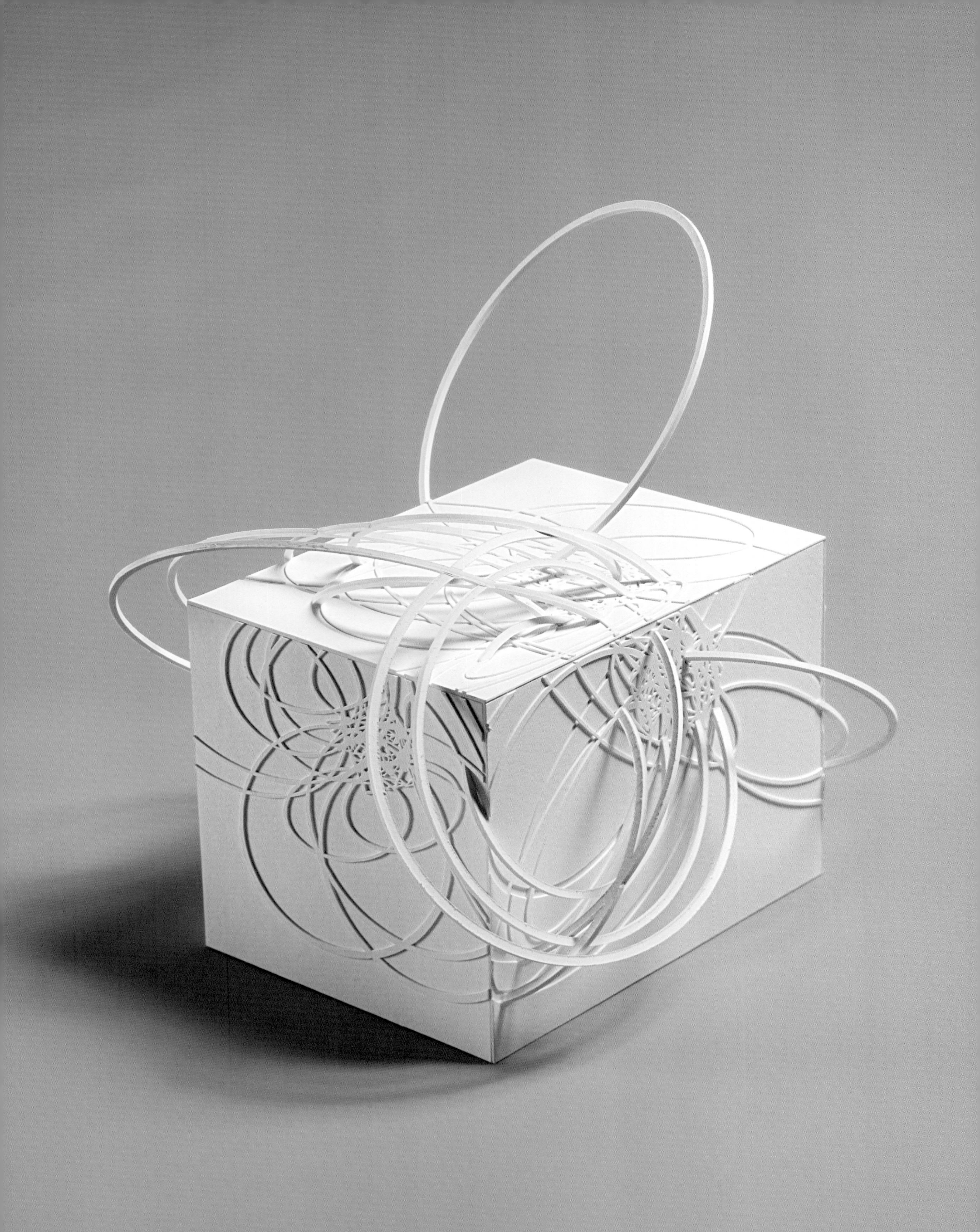

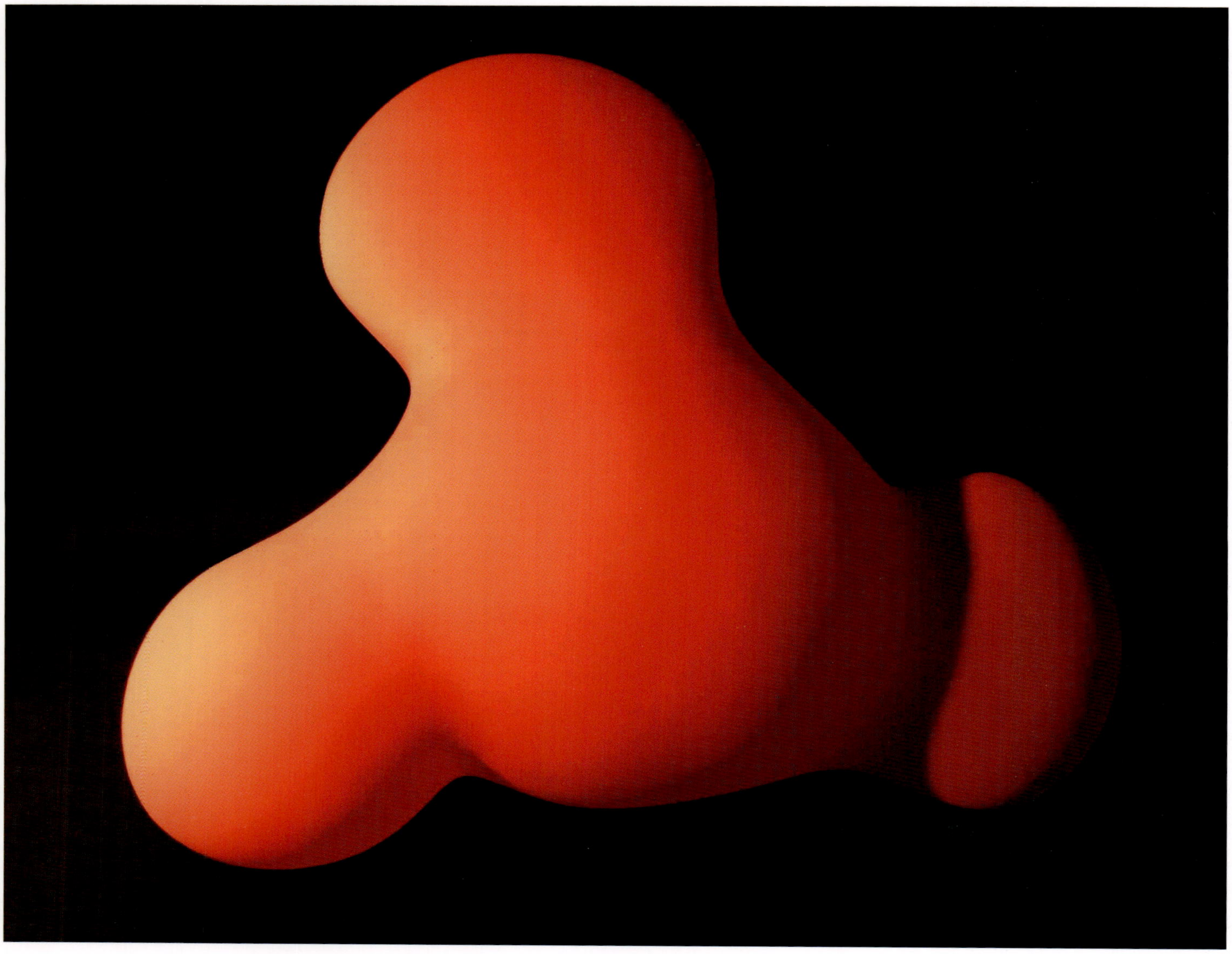

Greg Lynn Greg Lynn FORM

On my very first visit to the Glass House, I was struck not so much by the transparency of the house but by its privacy and contextualism. The brick walls running across the site through the fields were matched by the brick platform that extended beyond the house's glass envelope. I remember Philip telling me that in the summertime the deer would come into the house at night to sleep. And of course there is the Glass House's companion in brick, which I have always associated with David Whitney, as well as with Andy Warhol, who was so famously photographed within. So my contribution to *Modern Views* is a new brick that I designed—a hollow, plastic brick that when cut with a robotic arm welds to its neighbors to form self-supporting "Blob Walls."

Richard Meier Richard Meier & Partners Architects

I recall a lunch Philip hosted at the Glass House with me and Jim Sterling and Peter Eisenman and Michael Graves. He preferred luncheons so that people could see the grounds and his collection. You couldn't hang art on the walls—there wasn't even a place for a toothbrush—so he built an underground gallery and hung his art. I loved Philip's precision of detail, the clarity of doing things well, not in terms of what he did but how he did it. I loved the minimalism of the house, the serenity of the place. I learned a lot from Philip, but I make sure you can hang art on my walls.

Helmut Jahn

Murphy/Jahn

One of Mies's greatest works was Farnsworth House. The Farnsworth was a revolution. It is a single space, a simple shelter, totally enclosed in glass, of the utmost transparency. It integrates with its natural setting and the seasonal changes. It challenges conventional living and, as a heroic piece of architecture, was ahead of its time.

Mies accomplished what nobody had done before in a house, making just one room, totally abstracting wall, roof, floor, and space. Enclosure and structure are totally integrated, and technology and environmental control pushed the limits of what was available. The Farnsworth House reaches such simplicity that nothing can be taken away from it, making it as perfect as a building can be.

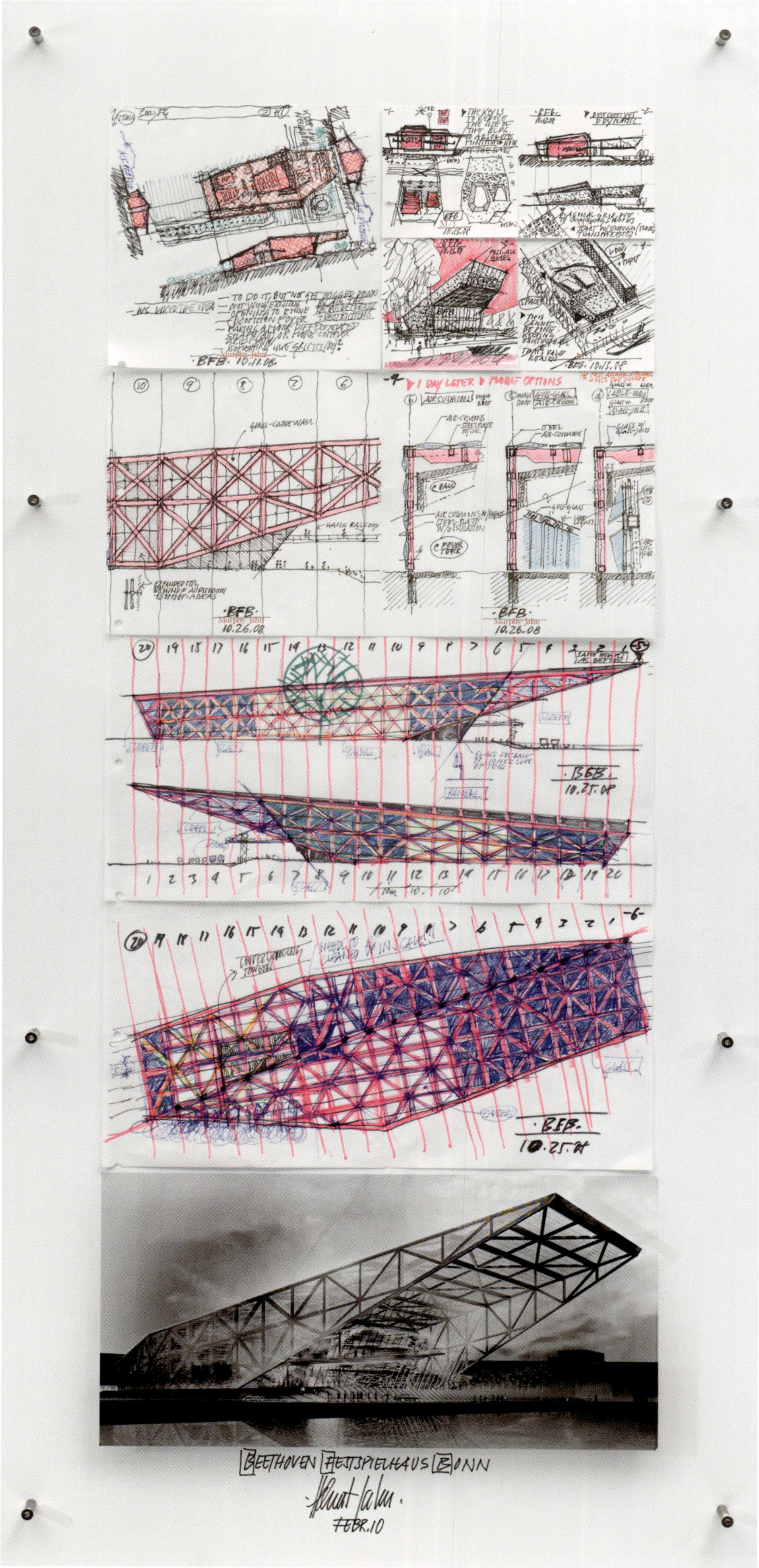

Patricia and John Patkau Patkau Architects

It is as much in their differences as in their similarities that the Glass House and Farnsworth House demonstrate the possibility implicit in the iconic Modern idea of a minimal enclosure of glass suspended between roof and floor. These two buildings represent a complex, at times contradictory, coincidence. Both are highly abstract, highly refined, and highly reduced; both are made of glass and steel. Yet each house embodies a very different idea of space. It is this difference, both in abstract conception and in concrete manifestation, between space as a discrete unit and space as a continuity, that reveals the individual identity of the architect within the universality of the idea.

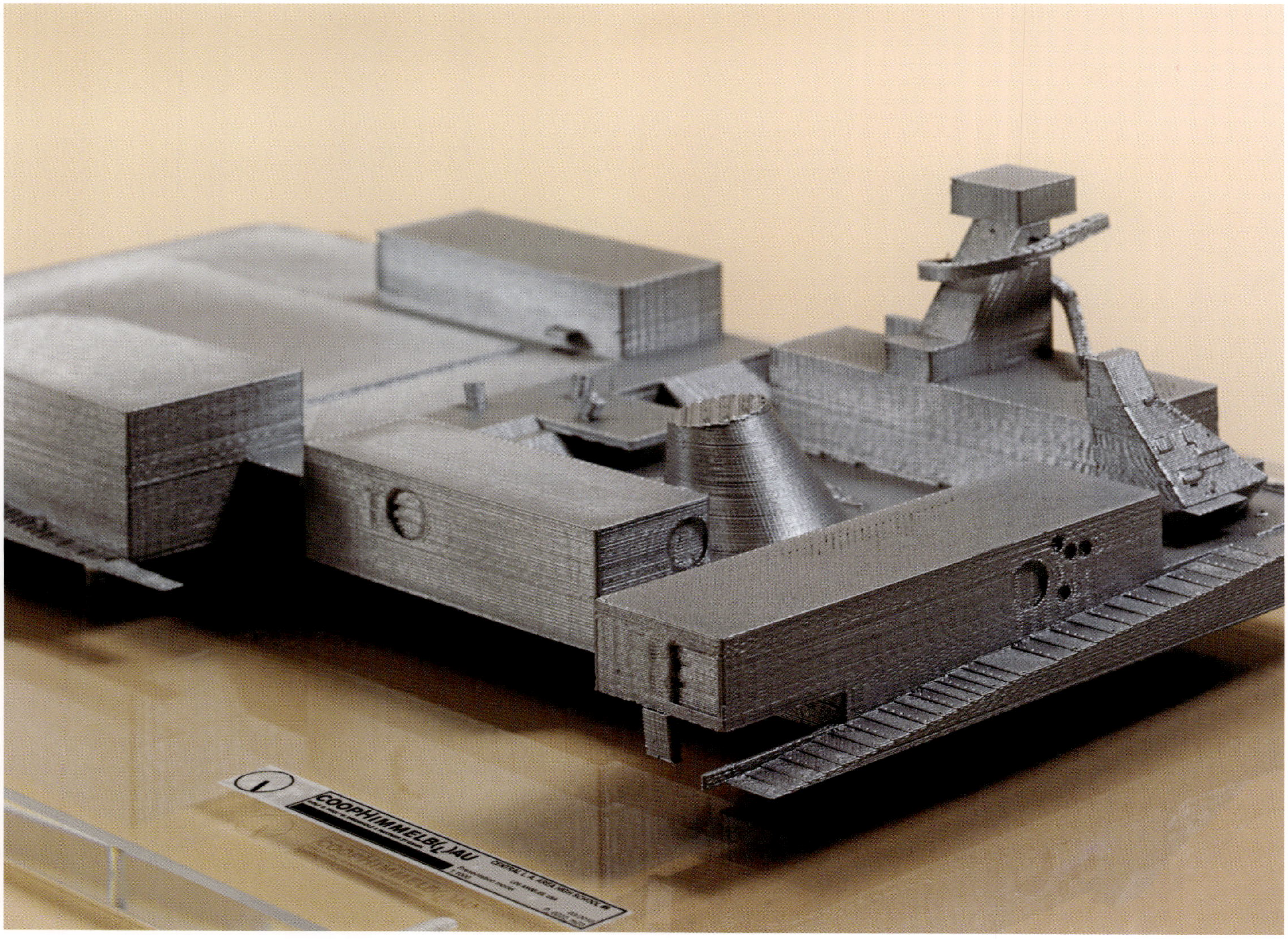

Wolf D. Prix **Coop Himmelb(l)au** ▲

Lebbeus Woods ▶

– 1981

Bernard Tschumi Bernard Tschumi Architects

We were asked in 1990 to design a viewing pavilion for a series of music videos. The organizers had in mind an opaque enclosure, all private, where visitors would see films in a small format on television screens. But we thought that it might be interesting to ask ourselves a question about the public nature of the program. It was in the center of Groningen, in northern Holland, and so it became an architectural manifesto about the nature of viewing.

We asked ourselves if we could build a building entirely out of glass, like Mies van der Rohe's Farnsworth House or Philip Johnson's Glass House, but do it in such a way that if the glass were removed there would be nothing left. With Mies or Johnson, if you take out the glass, the house is still there: the structure, the roof, and the mullions still define the presence of the house. So we thought, Could we take it one step further? We wanted to find a way to make the supports and beams entirely out of glass, so that the whole building would be simply a series of glass planes arranged to be held by clips: the ultimate glass house.

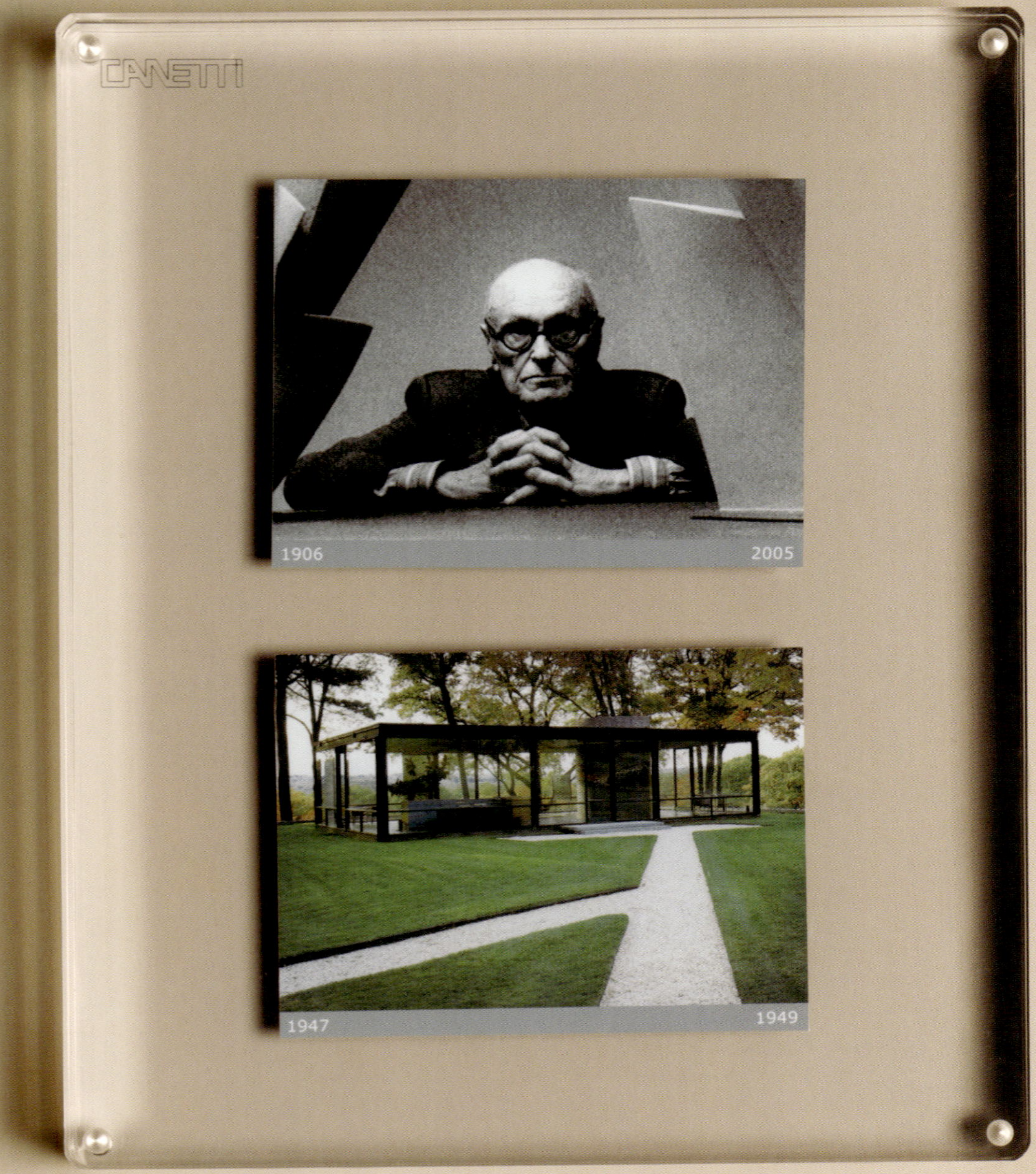

Jaquelin T. Robertson Cooper, Robertson & Partners

Johnson and Mies were classical modernists. One looked back and forward; the other changed the course of architecture. Think of Mies as the hedgehog and Johnson as the fox (a reference Johnson would have known—and Mies would not).

The Glass House is historically and physically grounded: its steel entablature and chair rails, brick plinth and drum, floating classical paintings, and symmetrical high doors bespeak its lineage; its glass and furniture, its modernity. It is both home and halo, a staged setting for an "entertainer" who shaped trends and reputations: historian, curator, collector, critic, teacher, political activist. Deeply committed, wildly successful, Johnson was a celebrity architect who, like Jefferson at Monticello, used his "little hill" as an "idea factory," a garden of architectural experimentations, excavations, and delights. He was, from the start, lord of his estate.

The Farnsworth House is *not* grounded, nor was it Mies's home or the centerpiece of his life. One of a number of reductivist pavilions, it floats—white, disembodied, purified—over a dangerous flood plain, a technically precise *hard* contact sited in a soft, leafy grove. It is a place for observing in which "life" is in service to "art" (i.e., it is better as an icon than a place to live)—the opposite of the Glass House. God is equally in its details and those of nature. It took a lord to raise it from the dead.

Bruce Kuwabara Kuwabara Payne McKenna Blumberg Architects ▲

This design for a house, located on pastoral farmland north of Toronto, is inspired by two modern houses designed by Mies van der Rohe: the Resor House and the Farnsworth House. The zigzag plan creates two L-shaped, open-ended courtyards at the front and back. The structure floats the ground floor as a platform for living over the gently sloping terrain. The front elevation is opaque and private, while the back maximizes floor-to-ceiling windows to open the interior to the landscape while simultaneously revealing the main living spaces as a tableau. Exterior walls are clad in long strips of Ontario limestone.

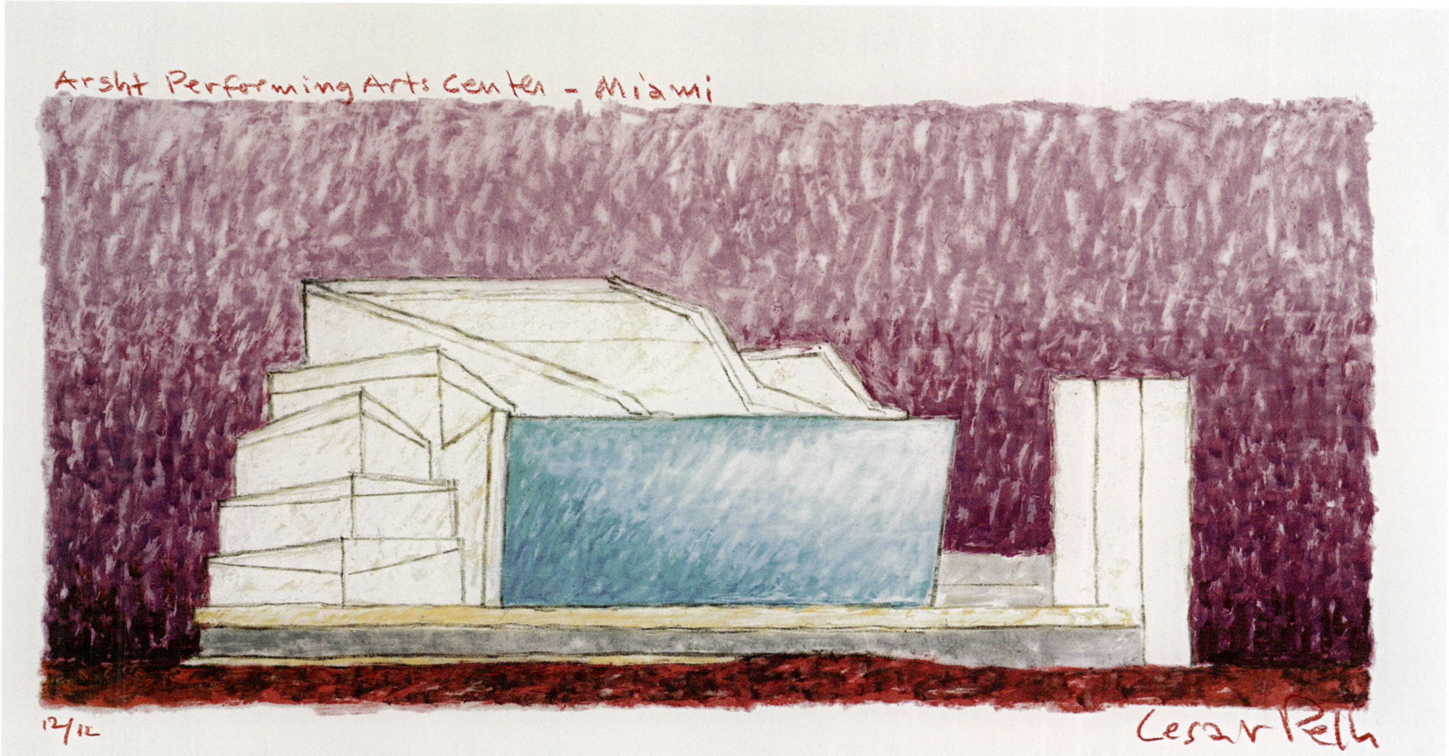

▼ **Mirko Zardini** Director of the Canadian Centre for Architecture
Lukas Meyer Studio Meyer Piattini

With the passage of time, Modernism has evolved from an ideology, a program that promised a totalizing unity, into a layer of the urban landscape. While Philip Johnson's Glass House and Mies van der Rohe's Farnsworth House are now monuments for historic preservation, so many elements of the Modern project retain central roles in our daily lives.

◀ **Cesar Pelli** Pelli Clarke Pelli Architects

I greatly admire Mies van der Rohe's Farnsworth House for its beauty, its intelligence, and its clarity of thought. It continues to be a model for many architects. I very much enjoy Philip Johnson's Glass House because of its livability and the pleasure one derives from being in it. Part of this sense of livability, of course, comes from the addition of the Brick House, which provides the privacy not available in the glass enclosure. Both houses are sheathed in glass, but they respond to two very different sensibilities.

Michael Graves Michael Graves & Associates

Philip Johnson once said, "You cannot *not* know history." Certainly Le Corbusier and Mies van der Rohe felt the same way. When we compare Farnsworth House with the Glass House, it is useful to broaden the historical view. Mies and Johnson of course knew Corbusier's free-plan Villa Savoye, but their interests lay in discovering how their own modern architectural language was both similar to and different from Corbusier's. Villa Savoye is well known for its columns that permit spatial divisions established by non-load-bearing partitions. In the Glass House and Farnsworth House, Johnson and Mies push the columns to the periphery, and like Corbusier, they employ non-load-bearing partitions to divide the interiors. Looking back in time at the Parthenon, we see a periphery of columns surrounding the central walls of the cella, a composition similar in intent to the spatial separations of both Johnson and Mies.
History is never a straight line but a path that, no matter how circuitous, architects must know.

Kenzo Tange Tange Associates

Pritzker Architecture Prize 1987 acceptance speech, Tokyo University

With de-emphasis on industrialization and the advent of the "information-communication society," the fundamentally rational and functional philosophy of the preceding period changed, and people sought things that appeal to the emotions and the senses.
In architecture, the demand was no longer for boxlike forms but for buildings that have something to say to the human emotions. That new demand has had an effect on the designs of everything, from small window displays to streetscapes to buildings....
There is a powerful need for symbolism, and that means the architecture must have something that appeals to the human heart. Nevertheless, the basic forms, spaces, and appearances must be logical. Designs of purely arbitrary nature cannot be expected to last long.

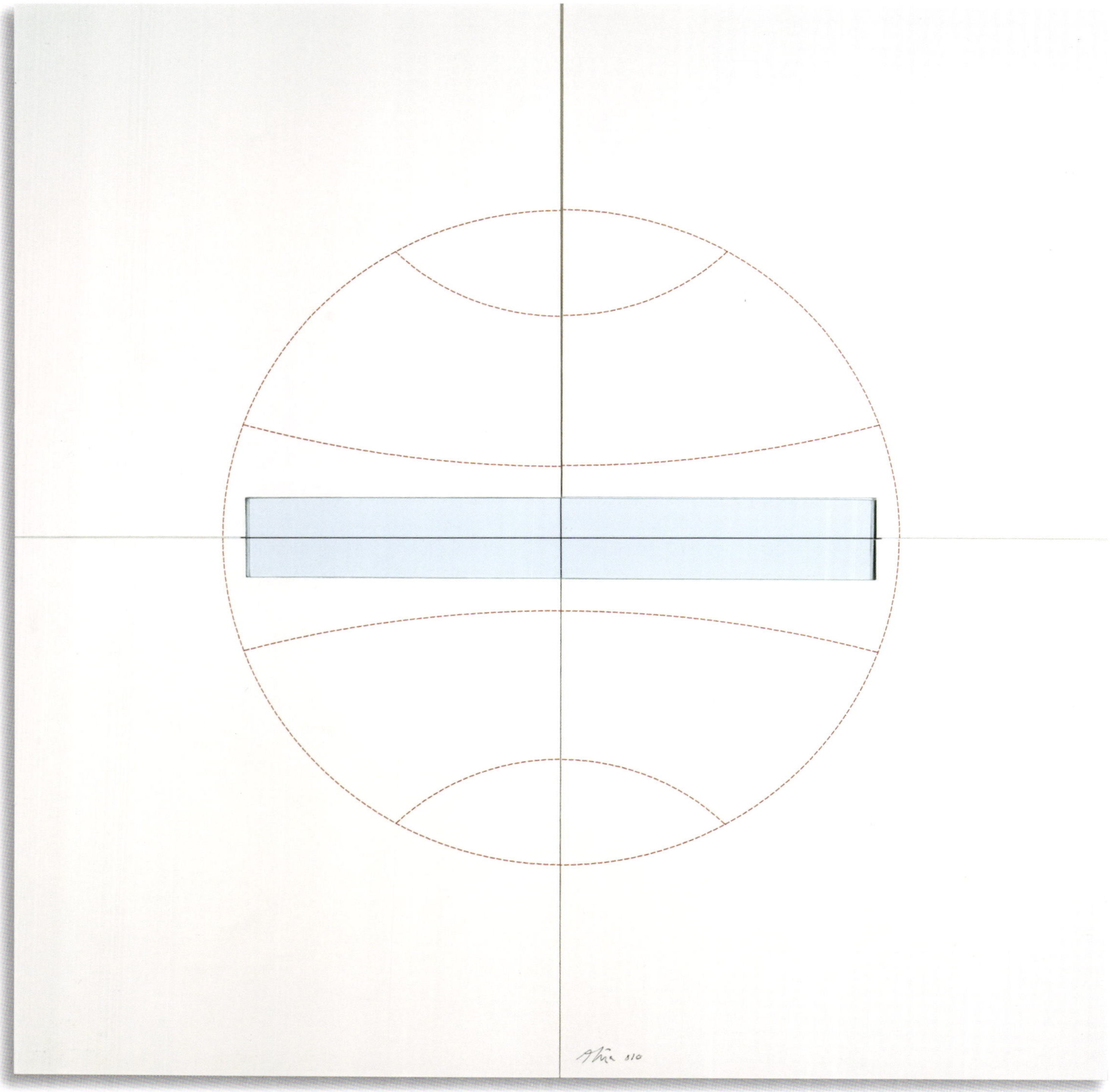

Álvaro Siza

What impresses me the most in Mies van der Rohe's work is the clarity of his classical education, which goes hand in hand with a profound sense of innovation. Both of them are present in the use of technology and in the frequent correlation, right at the roots of his architecture, between the ancient and the contemporary. Mies's blueprint for his Brick Country House (near Potsdam, 1924), for example, brings out his rapport with Frank Lloyd Wright's architecture, just as the white vision of Farnsworth House bears the singularity of a Greek temple.

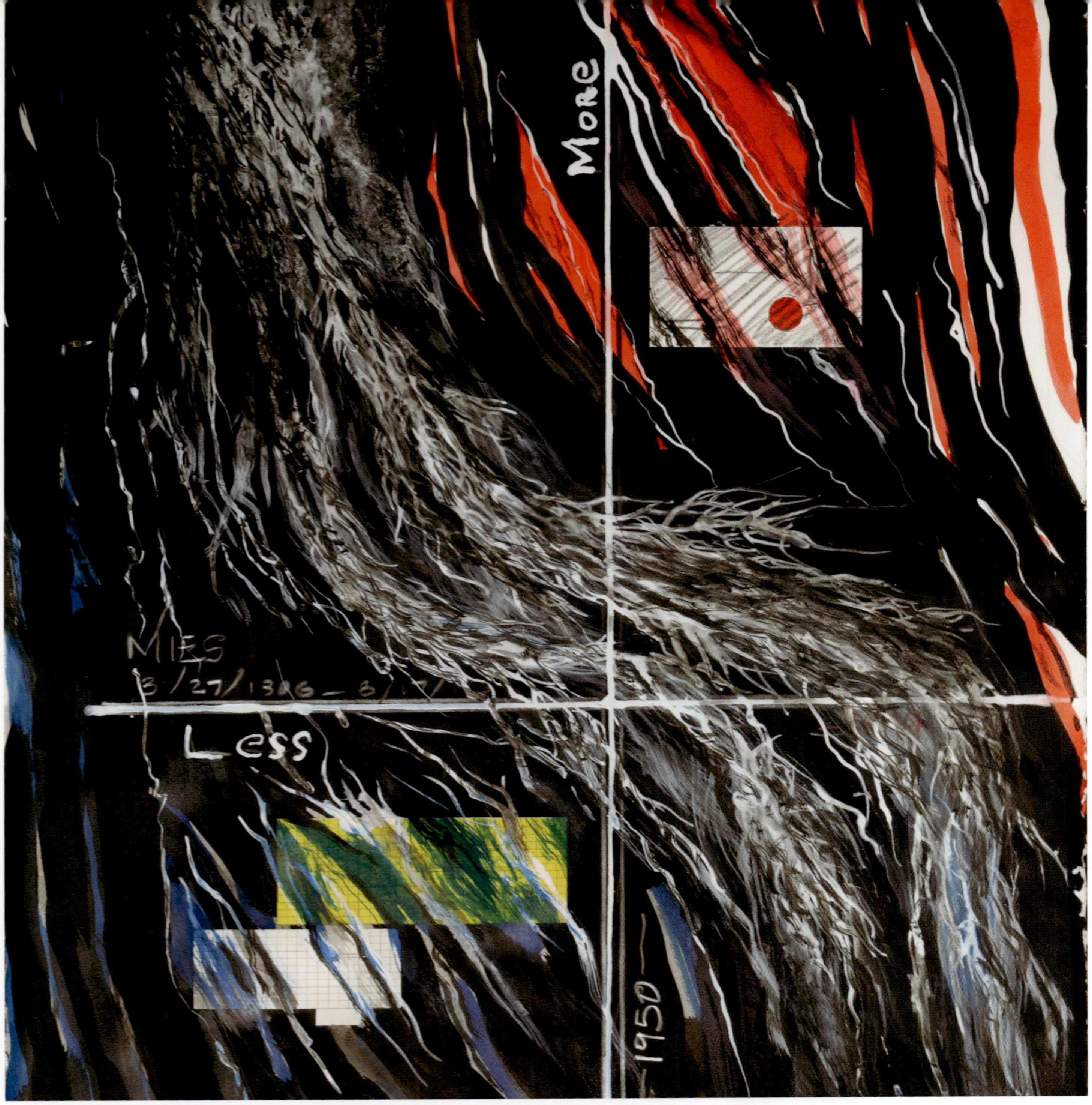

Adrian Smith **Adrian Smith + Gordon Gill Architects**

"Go instead where there is no path and leave a trail."
—Ralph Waldo Emerson

Ludwig Mies van der Rohe exemplified this spirit but stopped to emphasize the singularity of his path. He has said that it is for others to explore alternative visions. His teachings and those who followed in his path strayed little from it. Not so with Philip Johnson, who explored many paths, most of which were well worn and few of which left a trail.

Both the Glass House and Farnsworth House exhibit a beautiful fundamental flaw: that of context. Each has its basis in observing the natural environment through the connectivity of its interior and exterior, but each fails to observe nature's forces of flooding and heat.

The paths are turbulent now, the direction uncertain—the trail is lost. "Sometimes blaze a new trail."

where do you rest your mind · where do your dreams becom
mysterious shift of light · when nature encounters huma
heaven · we step outside to gaze at stars · at star

Tod Williams and Billie Tsien Tod Williams Billie Tsien Architects

reality · is it the torque of day and night · a
kind our minds drift in and out · imagining
then back inside to warm our souls

Stanley Tigerman **Tigerman McCurry Architects**

Letter from Stanley Tigerman to Mies van der Rohe, 1978

Dear Mies:

The state of architecture has grown curiouser and curiouser in the ten years you've been gone. There's something called "postmodernism" now, which seems to be getting everyone's attention. I guess it means to be something more than just "after Modern architecture," which is not to suggest that there aren't even those who think Modern architecture failed. Can you believe there are even mutterings about the death of Modern architecture? But don't worry—it's very much alive.

Love,

Stanley

Calvin Tsao

Tsao & McKown Architects

How do you turn a corner? The question engaged Donato Bramante at Santa Maria Della Pace and, in our time, Mies van der Rohe at Farnsworth House. Facing the diametrical spirit of tradition and classicism, Mies and his contemporaries sought to define and craft the Modernist movement mainly in terms of what Modernism was not. With an adventurous view toward a new future, Modernism cast off the heavy ornamentation mandated by centuries of aesthetic dogma, of tradition. Yet it also declared and embraced a commitment to the essential platonic ideals of its classical antecedents: to reveal nature's inherent logic and sense of order, and to attain visual and spiritual harmony.

Ron Radziner **Marmol Radziner**

I have always been intrigued by the way the Glass House and Farnsworth House are situated against a dense landscape, creating a conversation among the rough texture of the woods, the manicured lawns, and the crisp lines of glass and steel. Yet most dramatically, my reflections on these iconic buildings have always centered on the dialogue of colors. Black and white, the two buildings seem to effortlessly speak to the greens, browns, and grays of nature. Through both transparency and reflection, the buildings make us more aware of the colors and shapes of the natural world that surround us—more so than if they had never been built. They reflect our ongoing exploration of modern living and how the unification of indoor and outdoor environments shifts our relationship to nature.

Richard Rogers **Rogers Stirk Harbour + Partners**

Philip Johnson's New Canaan house is a simple glass rectangular container extremely carefully and consciously sited in the landscape. It is elegant and understated. No one part is dominant. The roof, the floors, and the walls seamlessly enclose the box, but don't be mistaken—every single item both inside and out is thoughtfully and beautifully positioned in relation to the other parts. It is perhaps low-key, especially when compared with Mies van der Rohe's Farnsworth House, where every plane and every piece of structure is clearly expressed and separated from each other in the most classical of manners. Both houses are transparent, but the New Canaan house is designed to be elegant and small, and Mies's is small but designed to look large and to stand proud.

My design for the Rogers' House in Wimbledon, which was inspired by these houses, tries to deal with additional contemporary problems such as growth and change, the standardization of components, and the conservation of energy. It is more of a robot and less of a temple.

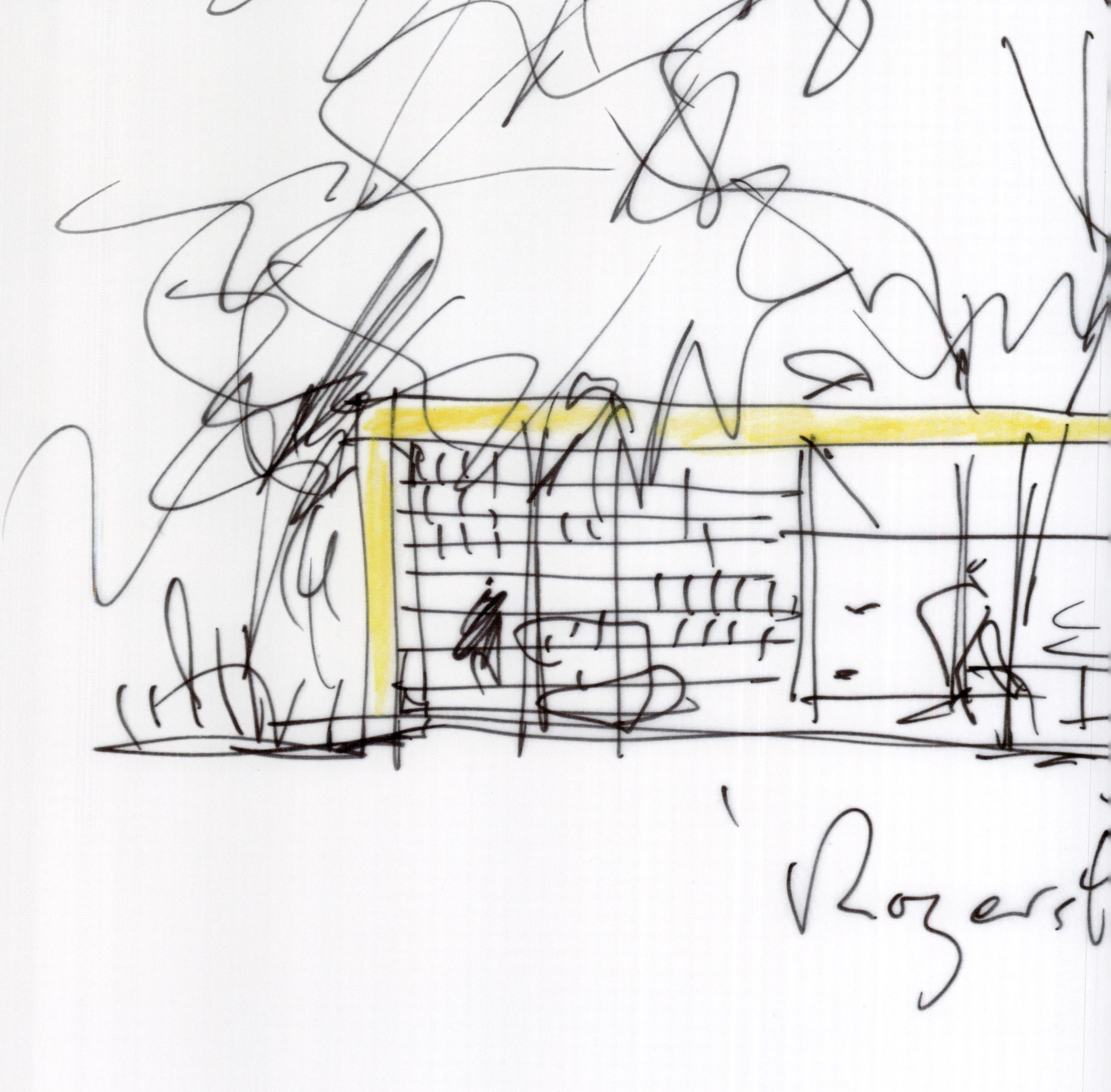

10
1
10
ouse

Dirk Lohan

Lohan Anderson

The Farnsworth House has been a presence in my entire life. I had pictures of it pinned up in my room as a teenager. I was fortunate to have stayed in it several times while I took care of it for the second owner, Peter Palumbo.
I renovated it in the 1970s and again in the '90s after major flooding.
Now that I finally have seen the Philip Johnson Glass House, I was immediately compelled to investigate the similarities and differences between these two icons. The idea popped into my head to merge, enmesh, and collide them in drawings and model form; a fascinating process that led me to recognize the nuances of the similarities and differences and made me realize how rich and varied Modernism is.

2. LANDSCAPE ARCHITECTS

Gary Hilderbrand

Gary Hilderbrand Reed Hilderbrand ▲

Almost Nothing recalls photomontages by Mies, notably for his unbuilt Resor House, in 1937. Mies describes the aim of reducing the presence of building to *beinahe nichts*, or almost nothing. The Farnsworth House and the Glass House exploit this motive. Over time, in both, the landscape becomes almost everything.
With apologies to photographers Eirik Johnson and Paul Warchol.

Walter Hood Hood Design ▶

Peter Latz Latz + Partner

The house is the garden; the garden is the house. The four "walls" are the trees and bushes beyond the grass, and swallows soar through the bedroom, the chirruping of the sparrows only slightly muted. Rain doesn't make you wet; there is no sense of cold or heat.

Inside it is always summer. Only one further thought: the membrane is immaterial—nothing but a bundle of rays and waves separates the inside from the outside.

Two buildings closer to nature than an Indian tepee, nearer to the vision of Modernism than anywhere else.

Diana Balmori Balmori Associates

I see the Glass House and Farnsworth House as buildings that give the visual illusion of disappearing and allowing landscape to pass through them, and they stand nearly alone in the Modern movement in that respect.
In my own work, I have been interested in the passage from building to landscape and vice versa, and have been seeking a visual form of representation and design that does not cut objects sharply out of their context, but expresses them as a continuum. I find both buildings quite miraculous in how they achieve the illusion of a continuum. I would like to go beyond the illusion.

Adriaan Geuze West 8 Urban Design & Landscape Architecture

Our firm believes that a vibrant city needs three things: good social interaction, good infrastructure, and nature, in one or another of her varied forms. The great nineteenth-century parks were a fulfillment of the promise of an urban nature—of

a sublime second nature—and were conceived of largely as an antidote to the ills of industrial-era cities. In the modern era, two contrasting sensibilities would come to reflect these differing priorities: what we might call "mechanics" and "organics." We now inhabit a rapidly urbanizing world—but civilization is based on agricultural life. So this fundamental challenge remains unresolved.

Kathryn Gustafson

The Farnsworth House and the Glass House are jewels of Modernism in their simplicity of line and form. They act as a stage from which the visitor can look outward toward the surrounding landscape, where the glass reflects the sky and the lush greenery. In this image of my Morbras Meeting Point, in France, I treated the land as a sculptural form surrounding the reservoir, a place where visitors can look outward from within the landscape and the pristine water reflects the clouds above. We often seek to create serenity, the time and space to reflect. We need places—both buildings and landscapes—to remove the excess, the nonessential, and give some semblance of clarity to the rest.

3. ARTISTS

Annie Leibovitz

Claes Oldenburg and Coosje van Bruggen

The Architect's Handkerchief

The handkerchief in the breast pocket has gone out of style, at least in the western world, but at one time it was the *sine qua non* of the perfect gentleman's dress. It survives as a symbol in the card slipped into the pocket of a suit when it is returned from our local cleaners, on Downing Street in New York City, a symbol that exploits the coincidence of its address with that of the prime minister of the United Kingdom.

In *The Master Builders*, Peter Blake wrote of Ludwig Mies van der Rohe: "He is, indeed, something of a dandy in a subdued way: there is generally a very soft, very expensive handkerchief trailing out of his breast pocket, and he obviously likes fine quality in all his personal belongings."

In fact, photos of Mies always show a breast-pocket handkerchief in a different arrangement, suggesting that it is not just an ornament. Perhaps he has just had to mop his brow, or maybe he wishes to signal his playfulness. We take it as a sign of the architect's state of mind, his invention. We liken it to the contrast Mies achieved when he placed a figurative sculpture in the geometrical environment of the Barcelona Pavilion at the 1929 International Exposition in Spain.

Our sculpture treats the handkerchief like a torch, the token of the bearer's inspiration. We represent it from two viewpoints: the one facing out, or the public side, and the other facing the person (the heart), or the private, backstage view. To give the subject more independence as a sculpture, it is tilted leftward, as no breast pocket would be, and the handkerchief emerges opposite to its proper direction.

NEW DOWNING S
CLEANER
"The Designers Choice
In Drycleaning'
We Collect & Deliv
(212) 255-622
OPEN:
Monday to Friday 7 a.m. to 7
Saturday 8 a.m. to 5 p.m.
- FOLD TO FIT POCKET -

Iñigo Manglano-Ovalle

Gravity Is a Force to Be Reckoned With is inspired by two uncompleted Modernist projects; Mies van der Rohe's House with Four Columns (c. 1951) and Sergei Eisenstein's screenplay *The Glass House* (c. late 1920s). Gravity is engineered as an inversion of Mies's theoretical house that in turn houses Eisenstein's film played back as a series of video phone messages to an absent protagonist. The engineering, building, and installation of *Gravity Is a Force to Be Reckoned With* was commissioned by Mass MoCA. This photograph, *Untitled Repose,* is a document of a series of ongoing performances that take place within and without the inverted dwelling.

Juergen Nogai + Julius Shulman

Julius Shulman and I sat together at the dining table in Philip Johnson's Glass House many times during our week-long stay. We would often sit silently enjoying the beauty surrounding us, and at other times engage in deep discussion about art and life, nature, people, and their passions—and, of course, Philip Johnson. During one of these talks Julius shared with me a lingering sadness. "I wish Philip could be here so I could share the beauty of his house with him, through my perspective as a photographer." But in the next moment he turned to me with a twinkle in his eye and said, "But you know...Philip Johnson has the most expensive wallpaper in the world!" Residing serenely in the rolling landscape, reflecting and flowing, the Glass House seems to derive its unending iconic power from the contradiction of its steel-and-glass structure with its chosen place. It is that very tension that makes it so exquisite, and challenges the sense of comfort one often searches for in a home. Trying to capture the spirit of the house is a quicksilver experience. While composing a shot, I often turned the camera to capture an expected angle, only to find myself provoked and seduced by the house itself through the constant play of reflection, light, and the nearly perfect lack of boundary between the landscape and the structure, life, and art

Louise Lawler

Jasper Johns's *Device Circle*, painted in 1959 and photographed in 1984 in the Connecticut home of Mr. and Mrs. Burton Tremaine, which was remodeled by Philip Johnson in 1952.

Richard Woods ▼

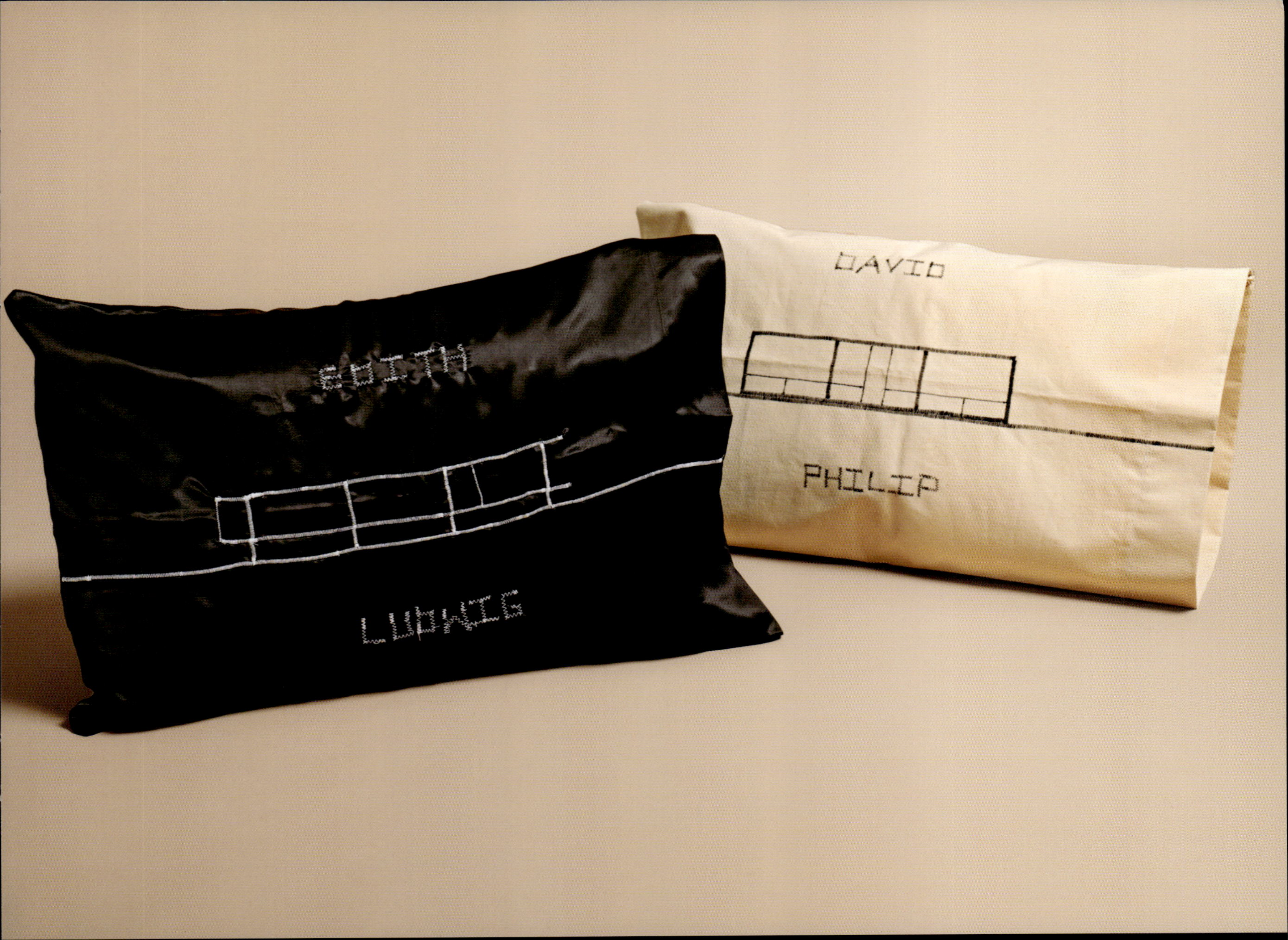

Fritz Haeg ▲

Since I am a student of architecture who came of age toward the end of the twentieth century, the Glass House and Farnsworth House are so deeply embedded in my subconscious that they seem almost inevitable. It is hard to imagine the unique human circumstances that created them and how they came alive when occupied as homes, with all of the eccentric intimacies that accompany real life. When I imagine the daily routine of Philip Johnson and David Whitney behind glass on that grassy knoll, and the intense meetings between Ludwig Mies van der Rohe and Edith Farnsworth on that perfect pedestal, these iconic structures of restrained classical virtues begin to reveal the messy truths of

Alessandro Twombly

Ken Price

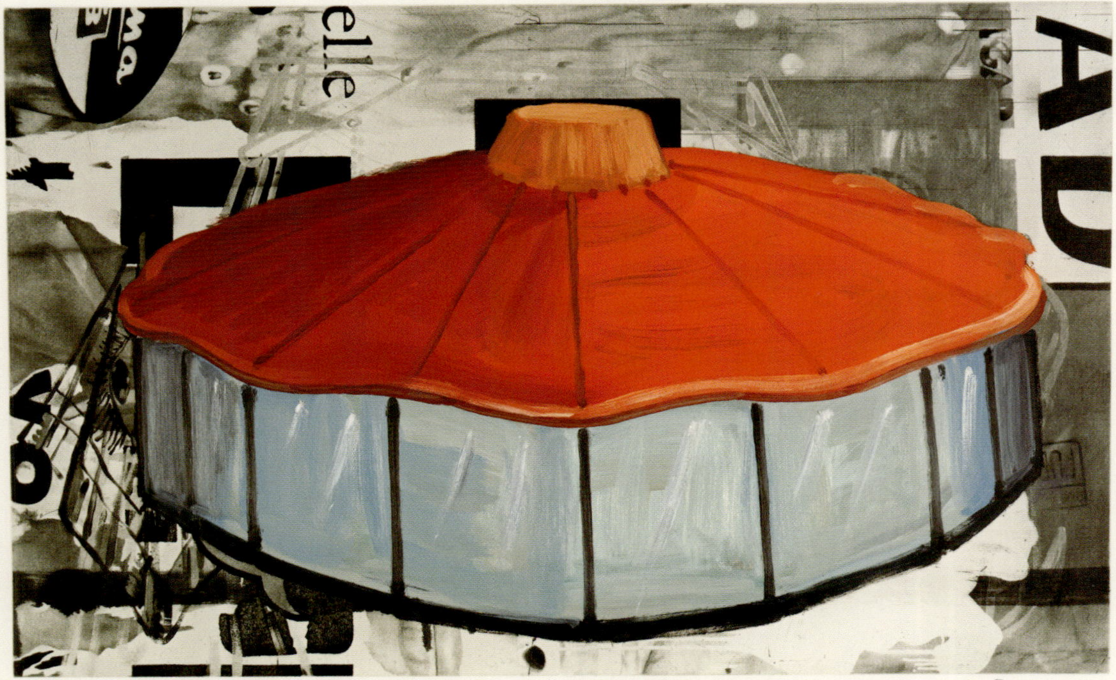
elle
AD

Maira Kalman

I came to the house on a sunny day. There were other houses on the grounds. In one, there was an ottoman and a bed. There was Fortuny wallpaper. In the main house there was a table. There was glass. There was a bird in the tree.There were many trees on the level ground. The ground was flat.There was a shedding of mass and trimming of being. A nice trimming.

Jaume Plensa

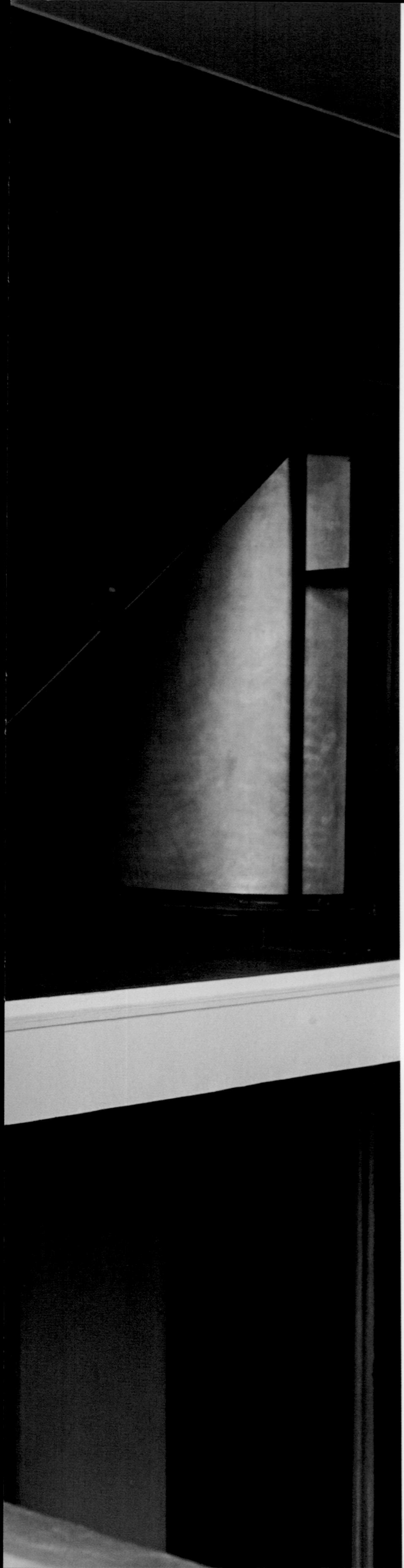

Lynn Davis

David Diao ▲

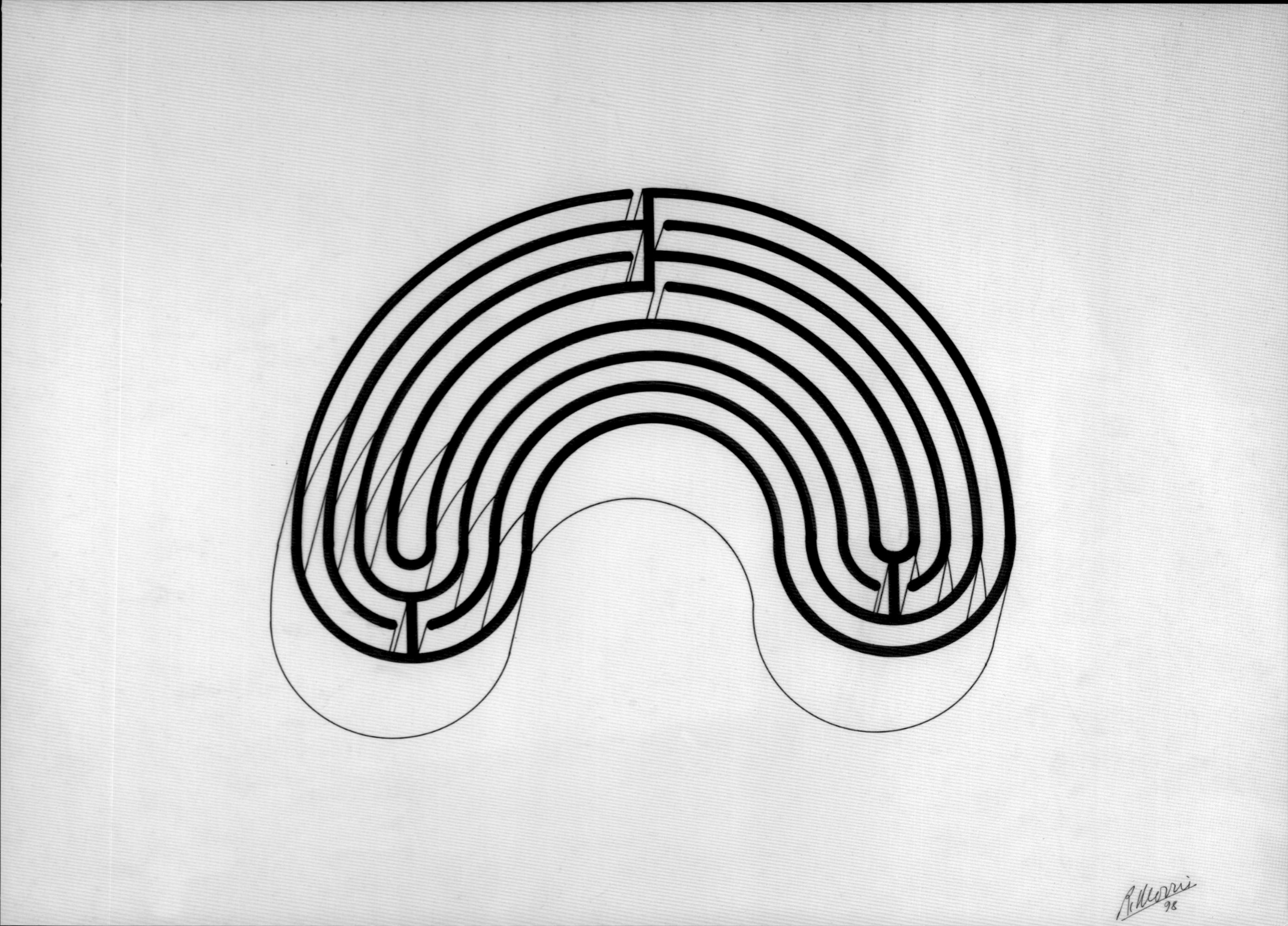

James Welling

James Rosenquist

In 1962, I met David Whitney when I had my first show at the Green Gallery on Fifty-seventh Street. David wanted to know if I needed a valet, meaning him.

In 1963, I met Philip Johnson, who asked me to do a mural on the New York State Pavilion at the 1964 World's Fair.

I would see Philip occasionally, bouncing around, signing drawings. I was invited to lunch twice at the Glass House, which was a very personal yet open experience.

Philip and David would come to my Christmas parties in the country. Philip was a very generous architect, giving praise to a number of his contemporaries. He was a large supporter of the arts. He bought a number of my paintings and built an unusual art gallery on the property where he could store many paintings on a big carousel, where you could select what you wanted to see. Later on he gave a great number of paintings to the Museum of Modern Art, but I think he kept his favorites.

Philip's Four Seasons restaurant in the Seagram Building is my favorite restaurant. It has high ceilings and enables one to think—besides having delicious food from Paul Kovi, Tom Margiattai, and Alex von Bidder. They asked me to do a painting for them. I painted a large one called *Fish, Flowers and Females* for the Four Seasons. It hung there for ten years and was given to the Metropolitan Museum when the building was sold.

Philip and David were very comedic, and I enjoyed their sense of humor. I wish they both were still with us.

sketch for TOSCA III
2010

Frank Stella ▲

Ed Ruscha ▶

Ed Ruscha 2009

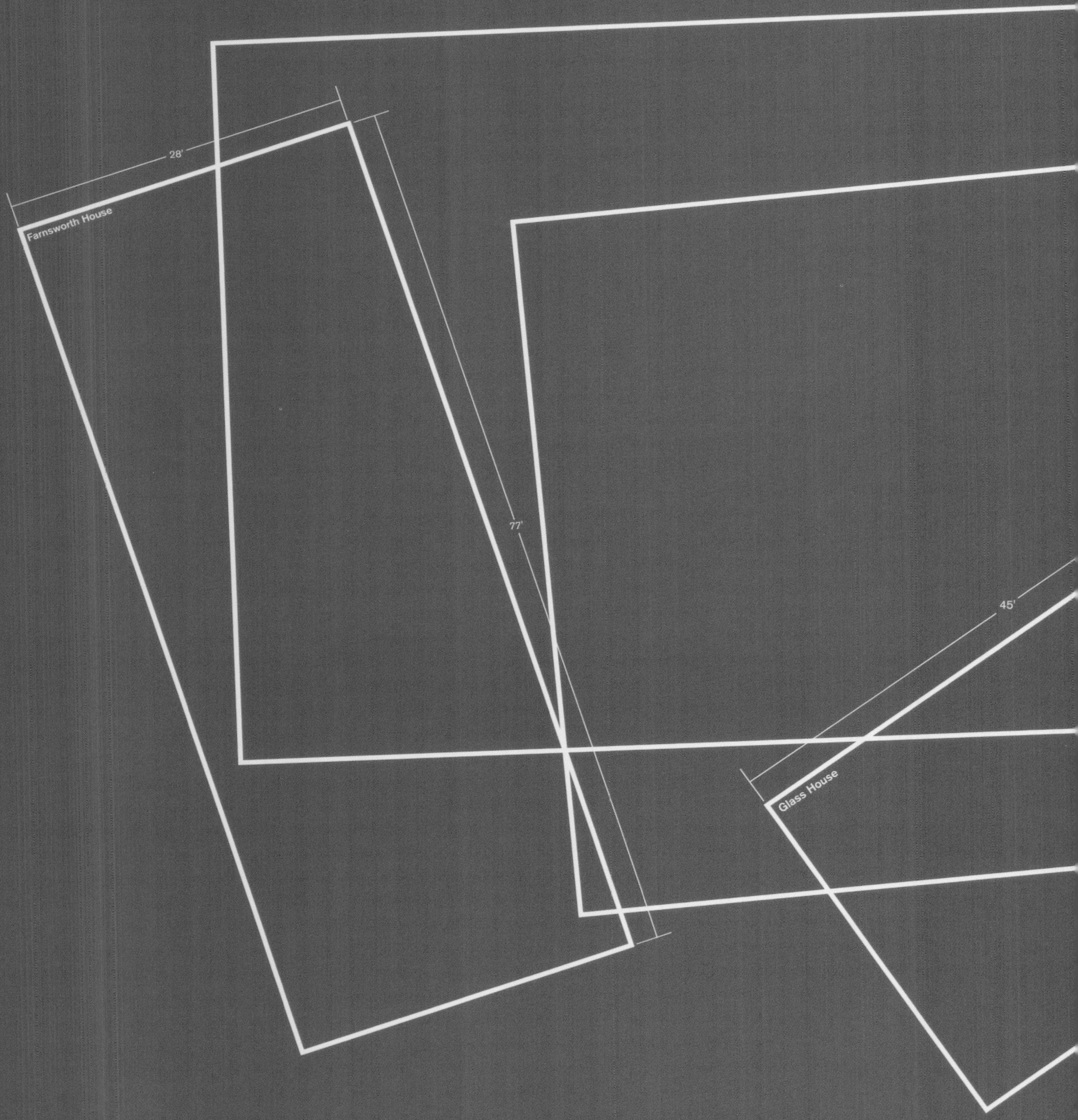
28'
Farnsworth House
77'
45'
Glass House

4. DESIGNERS

Paula Scher Pentagram

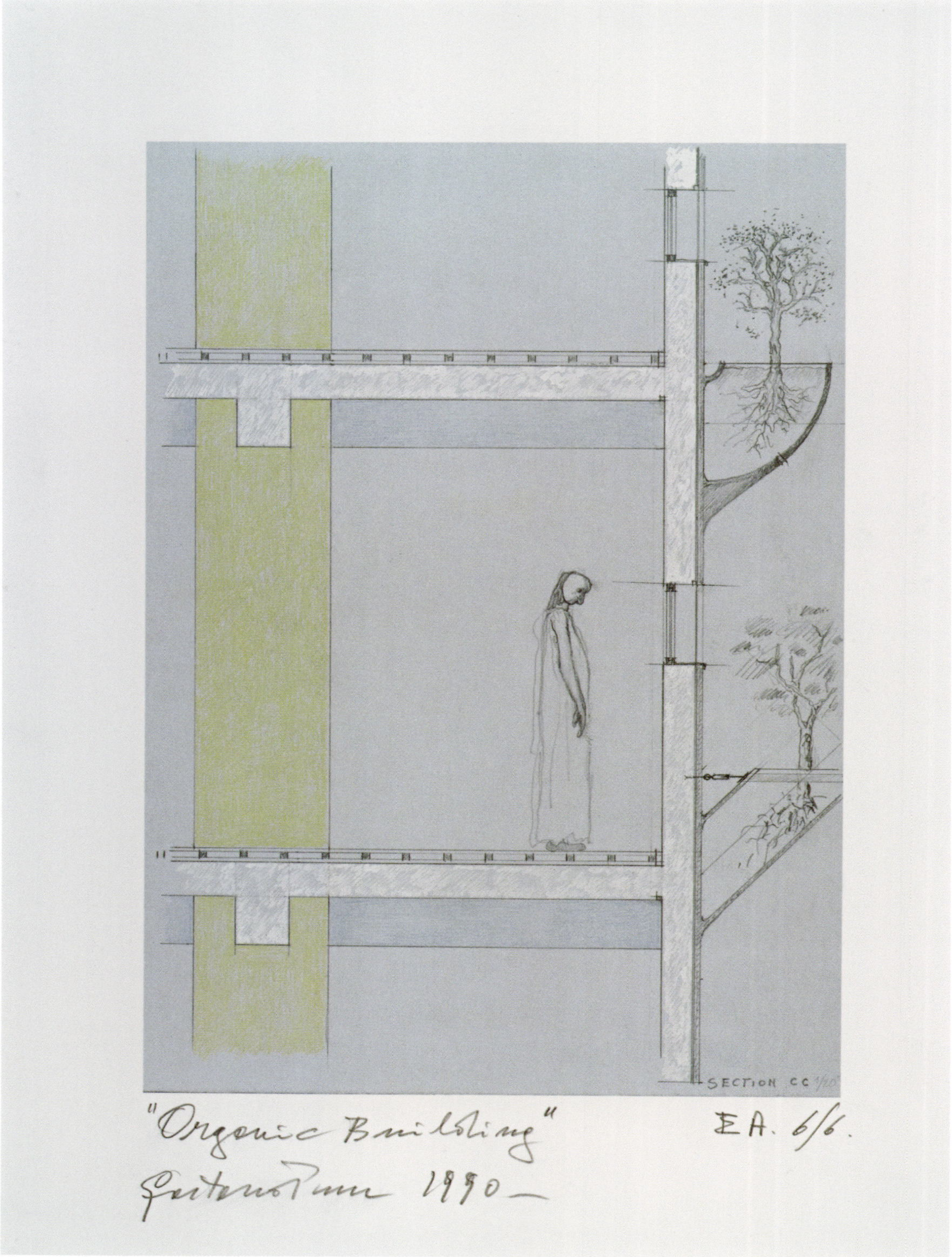

Gaetano Pesce

The Modern movement in architecture was authentic, because it was consistent with its historic context and because those architects expressed the needs of the society of their time. They conceived a uniform architecture that could be placed in any site, a kind of building elevated above any consideration of a locus and its particular characteristics, such as local culture or geographic position. This was known as the International Style. Today's architecture must be composed of differences, not homogeneity or uniformity. Architects must fight against the anonymity and sterilization of cultures and wage to do the opposite: enrich and develop them.

Karim Rashid

I was brought up with the prophecies of Modernism from Walter Gropius to Mies van der Rohe. My education was Teutonic Bauhausian. Reductiveness and plutonic geometry were sacred. But over the years I intentionally either softened or juxtaposed Modernism's purity, trying desperately to humanize it. I felt a need to create a more organic spirit in objects of everyday life. The Dekon table, although completely linear and minimal like Farnsworth House and liberally transparent like Philip Johnson's Glass house, is an object we look through and at, whereas both iconic houses have transparent vistas outward.

The Dekon table designed for the Italian firm Tonelli was an exercise of what I would refer to as distorted minimalism. Cut from a single sheet of tempered glass, the table consists of skewed planes that are mitered and UV-bonded to create two long floating glass surfaces. The table is composed of six glass planes, all unalike rhombuses, transparent and ethereal, deconstructing Modernism like Daniel Libeskind in the next generation of architects. Yet I see this table as a perfect object to exist in and complement both houses.

Ronan and Erwan Bouroullec

Both the Glass House and Farnsworth House represent for us a certain form of delicacy, a feature that is quite unexpected when we think about any type of constructions. This contradiction has been fascinating us throughout the years.

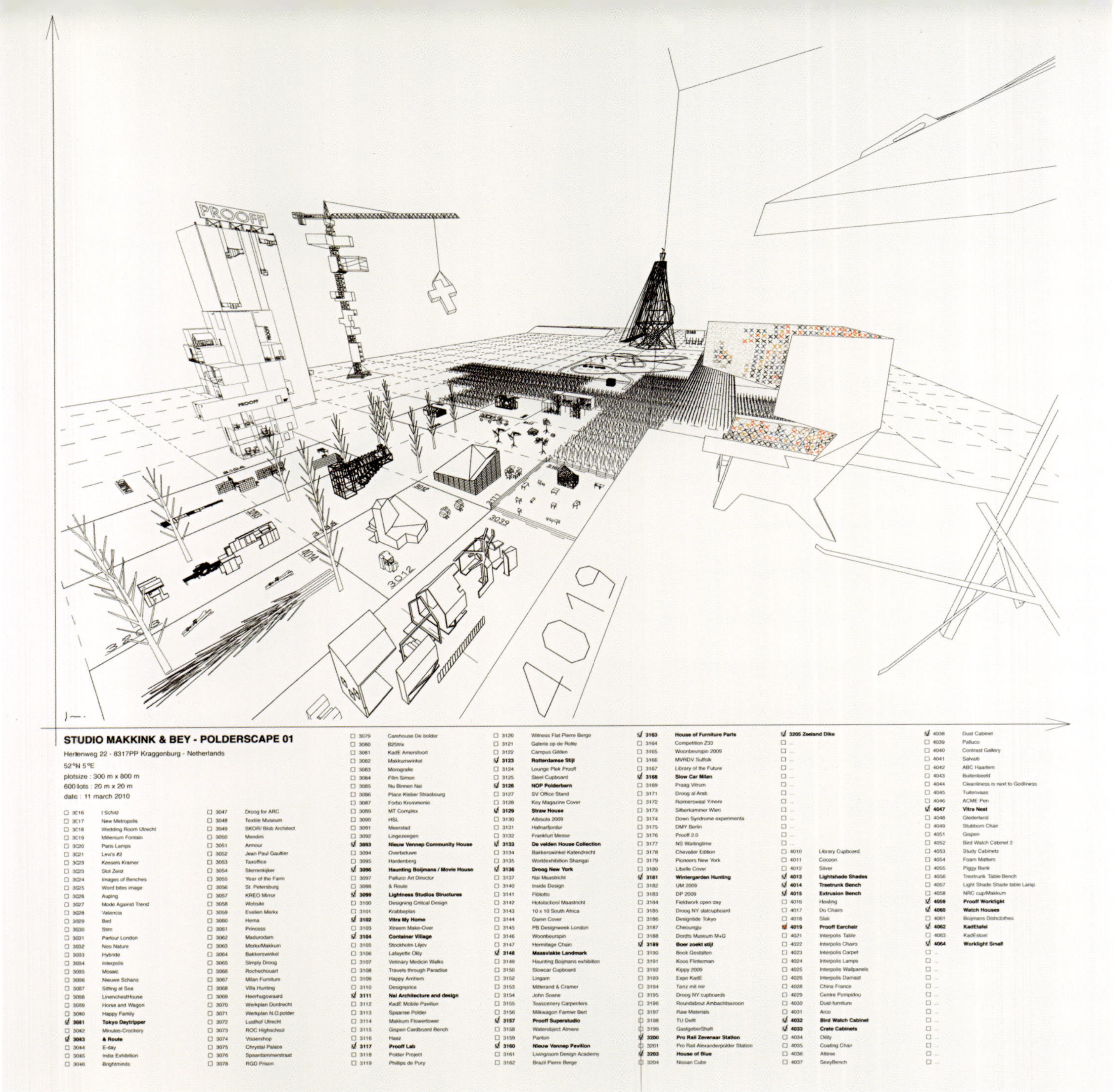

Studio Makkink & Bey

Studio Polderscape

One could assume that the Glass House on the estate in New Canaan was built to model the world according to Philip Johnson, as a test field where pavilions nest inside the landscape. The Glass House works as a viewing platform for carefully placed spatial experiments and the art collection. Here, inside and outside converge into something bigger, an isolated utopia of possibility. Studio Makkink & Bey tries to connect elements of different scales and from different origins to create well-tailored utopias. Studio Polderscape shows a drawing of a typical Dutch *polder*, a gridded topography closely resembling its real-life rendition. Our studio's projects—products, small pavilions, furniture, and public spaces—sit inside this diagram, each on its own plot of virtual land, to form a library. This virtual library provides a basis for new concepts for social design.

Maarten Baas

Where There's Smoke

Mattia Bonetti

Table Garden is defined by the characteristics, building typology, and aesthetics of the Glass House and Farnsworth House. My idea was to deconstruct the principles of the design of these two marvelous constructions: their transparency and the omnipresence of the natural environment. To do so, instead of constructing a small transparent space in the middle of natural surroundings, I constructed an enclosed perimeter completely occupied by vegetal elements. It is as if a garden had grown inside an abandoned Modern house, demonstrating the power and force of nature. The clay earth shaped by hand was perfectly suited for the predetermined purpose. To preserve the transparency, I added two acrylic walls. The earth, the grass, perhaps even flowers represent nature.

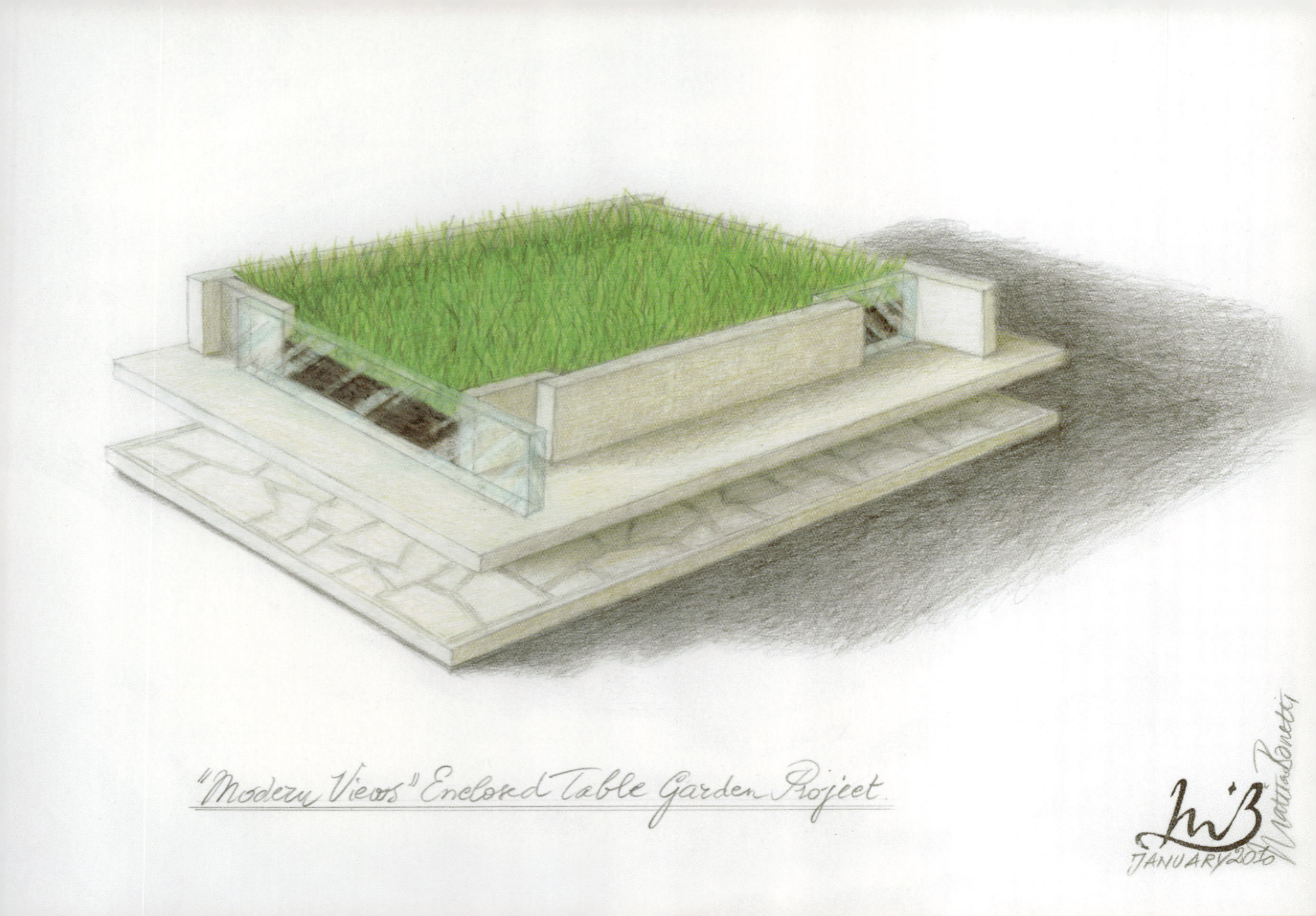
"Modern Views" Enclosed Table Garden Project
Mattia Bonetti
JANUARY 2010

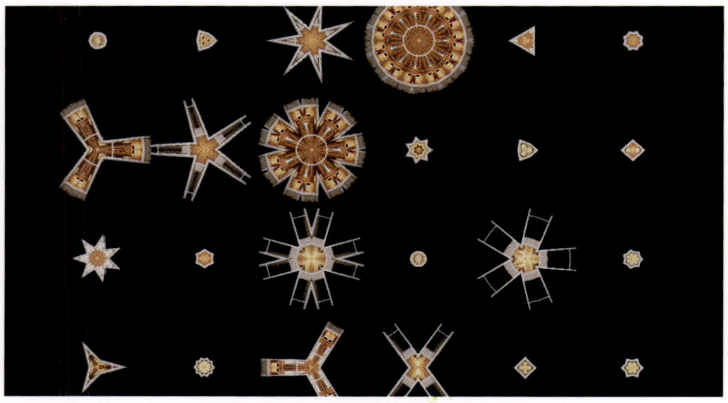

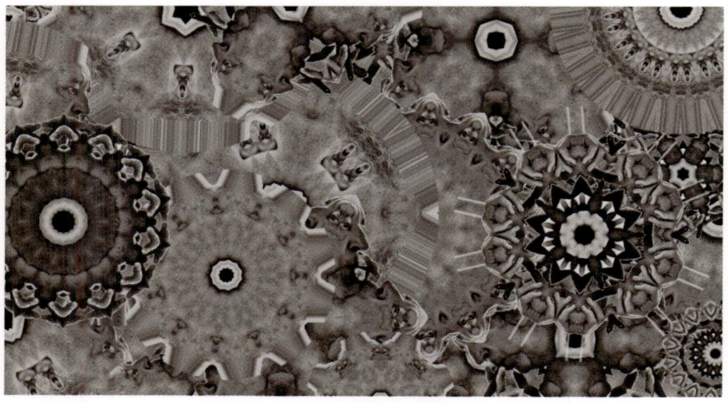

2x4

If the Farnsworth and Glass Houses are examples of a certain hyperrationality (at least in the architectonic sense), and their beauty is a by-product of a process rather than an end itself (according to Mies), could a hyperrational process be coaxed to produce an ecstatic, unintended beauty that surpasses the aesthetic imagination of the designer? The algorithm may be the apotheosis of rationality. Design, such as it is, is transformed into a set of instructions, lines of

dispassionate code, that dutifully complete a designated set of operations. The designer is separated from the design by a wall of ones and zeros. Data is fed in one end—in this case various and sundry images, plans, sections, and perspectives of these two iconic houses, as well as equally iconic portraits of their builders—the machine crunches the numbers, and out comes a steady stream of automatic design. The actual form, then, to get back to Mies, "is not the goal but the result of [the] work."

Constantin Boym Boym Partners

Over the years, we have created many miniature buildings inspired by the icons and events of the twentieth century. All along, I was imagining a seemingly impossible task of making something full-size, a monumental megasouvenir of Modernism.

Steel columns and beams are not merely structural components of the Mies van der Rohe and Johnson houses. In their uncompromising industrial clarity, these steel elements become an expression of the very essence of these buildings, icons of Modern architecture in their own right.

Souvenir of Modernism is a full-size fragment of an eight-inch H-column, a structural support exposed around the perimeter of Farnsworth House. The object is rendered to resemble a bronze monument, a timeless representation of classic modern elegance and simplicity.

2010

Vladimir Kagan Vladimir Kagan Design Group

The Mies van der Rohe Farnsworth House and the Philip Johnson Glass House are the quintessential role models for the modern house. Farnsworth is pure minimalism, using elegant materials and symmetry. Its captivating simplicity has cast a spell on architects for over half a century. There is a strong connection between the two houses. Mies's open plan and exposed steel were the big inspiration for Philip Johnson. The Glass House is the product of an aesthete who is building for his own life: Johnson was an experimenter influenced by diverse styles. His versatile creations often defy identification with their creator. His *joie de vivre* is evident in the diverse buildings he spawned on his extensive estate.

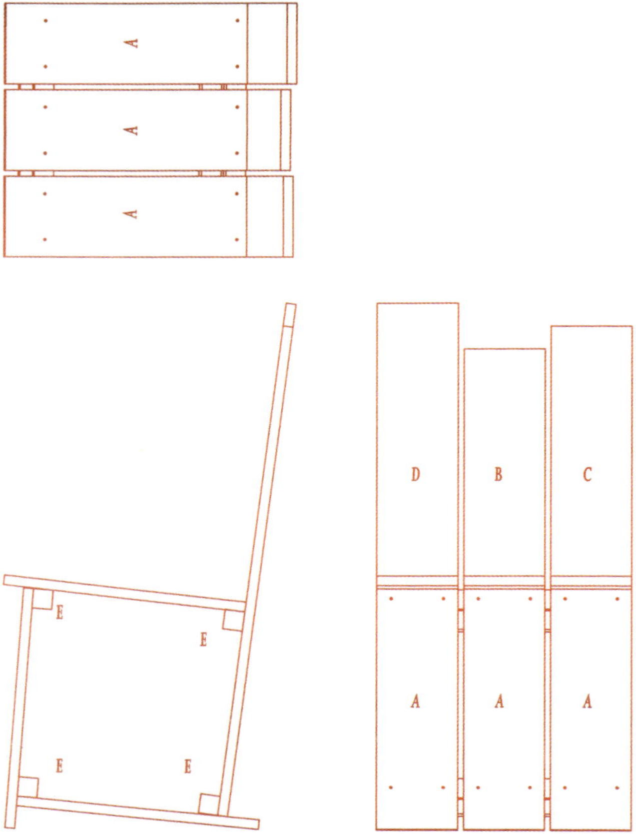

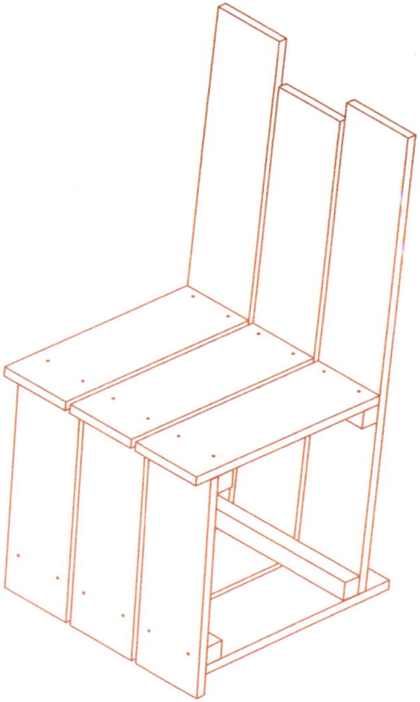

100023

	SEZIONE	LUNGHEZZA	QUANTITA
A	140 x 18/20mm	410mm	9
B	"	820mm	1
C	"	860mm	1
D	"	900mm	1
E	34 x 34mm	440mm	4

Martino Gamper

sedia db

...Revisited | A3

SCALE:1:2 | SHEET 1 OF 1

Jens Risom

Sheila Hicks *Diagonal*

Drawing a pliable line into tension
stretching it between distant anchor points
invites adventure.
Once the line, in the form of a strand of wool,
extends and doubles back—retracing its path—
a series of parallel warp threads assemble.
If the pliable line of a strand of wool
twists 45 percent to interlace and weave into the warp
It acts as weft.
Warp and weft activated

Mario Bellini Mario Bellini Architect(s)

Distilled Perfection of Transparency

Hidden in pastoral settings, the Glass House and Farnsworth House express the essence of modern dwelling: geometric form, simplicity, the beauty of proportion, glass walls (or, better, "air" walls), no decoration. Decoration comes instead from the outside green landscape—Johnson said it was difficult to read in the Glass House because the natural scenery around him was distracting. These two houses celebrate "open plan" living spaces. Refreshing and innovative, they express freedom, openness, circularity: the potentiality of multi-discipline-ness. Still, they sit solidly on the ground: witness the imposing cylinder of the Glass House! But both, borrowing some memorable words of Thoreau in *Walden*, "Lying between the earth and the heavens, [they partake] of the color of both."

Demian Repucci Lovegrove & Repucci

AMERICAN MODERNISM
THE FIGHT FOR THE TITLE CONTINUES!
PHILIP
JOHNSON
VS.
MIES
VAN DER ROHE
SQUARING OFF TO PRESERVE GREAT DESIGN
NATIONAL TRUST FOR HISTORIC PRESERVATION

Ludwig Mies van der Rohe, Farnsworth House. Elevation, plan, 1945–51.
Pencil on notepaper, 6" x 8 1/2" (15.2 cm x 21.6 cm).
© The Museum of Modern Art, New York.
The Mies van der Rohe Archive.

5. PLANS
Farnsworth House

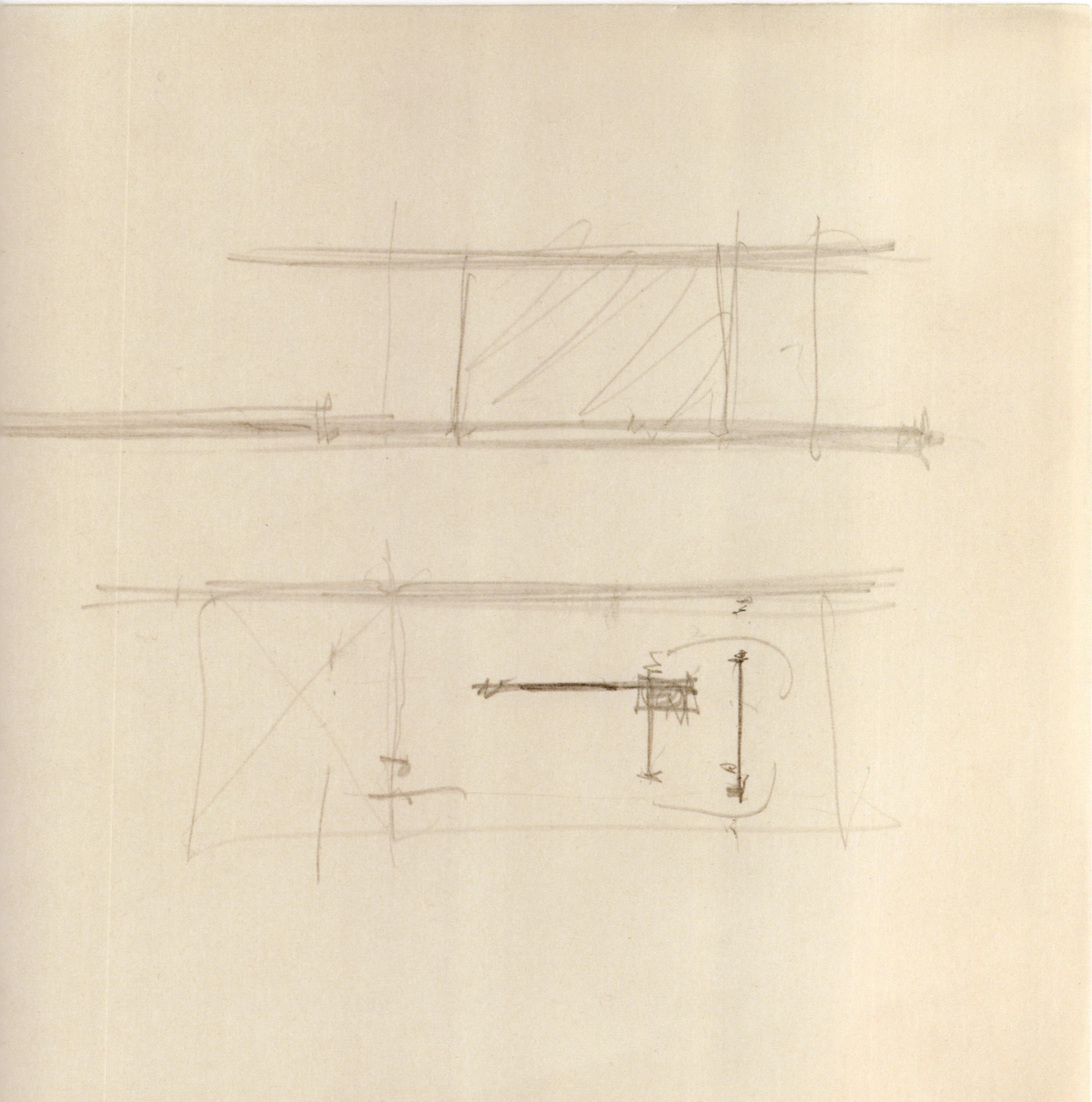

Ludwig Mies van der Rohe, Farnsworth House. Plan, sections, 1945–51.
Pencil on notepaper, 6" x 8 1/2" (15.2 cm x 21.6 cm).

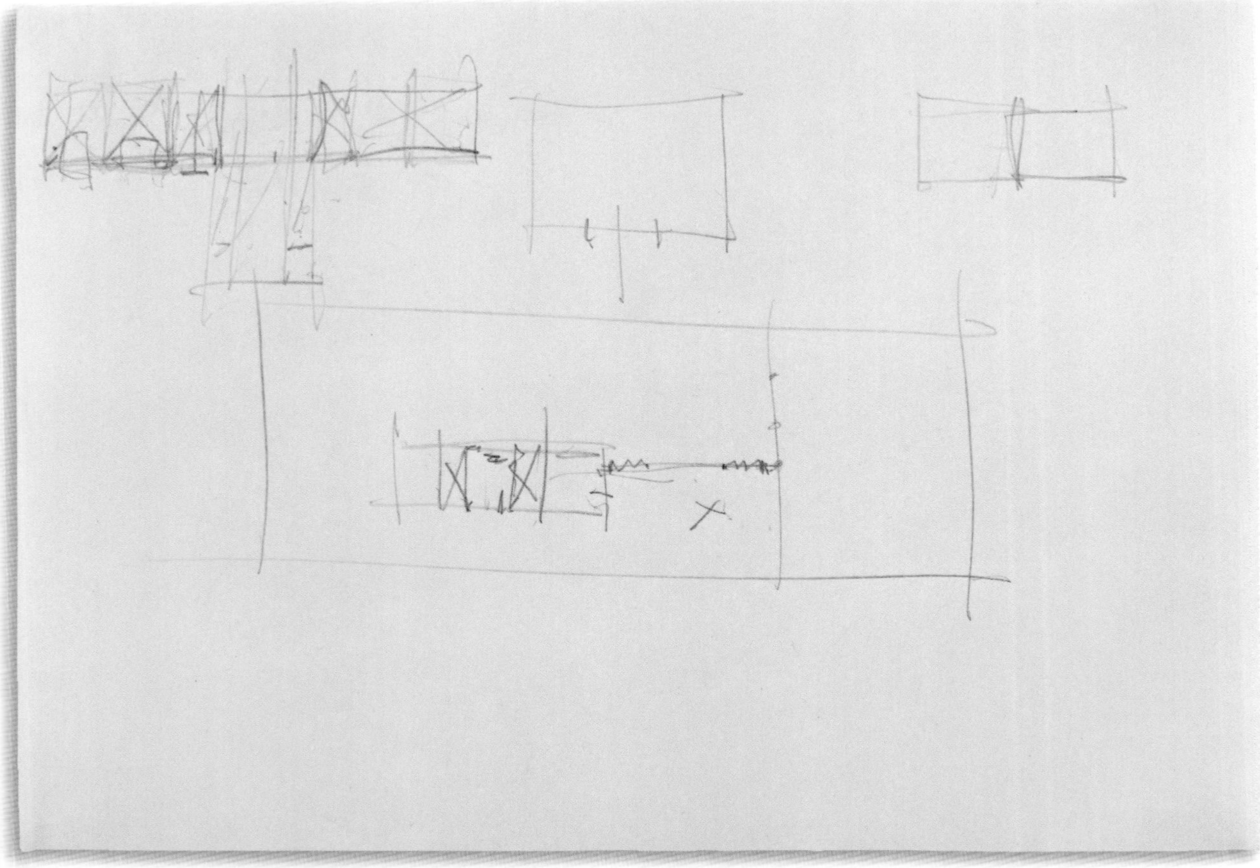

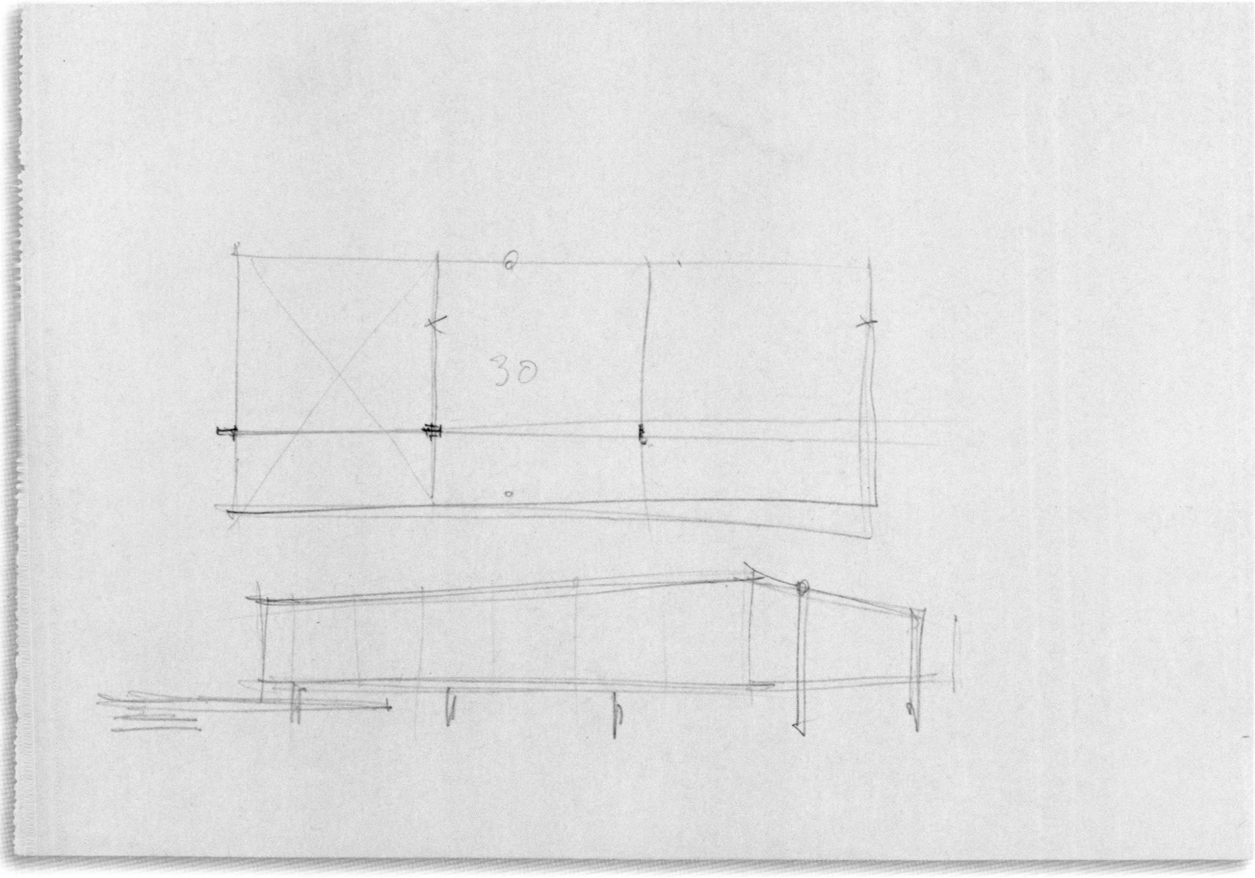

Ludwig Mies van der Rohe, Farnsworth House. Plan, exterior perspective, 1945.
Pencil on notepaper, 6" x 8 1/2" (15.2 cm x 21.6 cm).

Ludwig Mies van der Rohe, Farnsworth House. Floor plan, 1945–51.
Pencil on notepaper, 6" x 8 1/2" (15.2 cm x 21.6 cm).

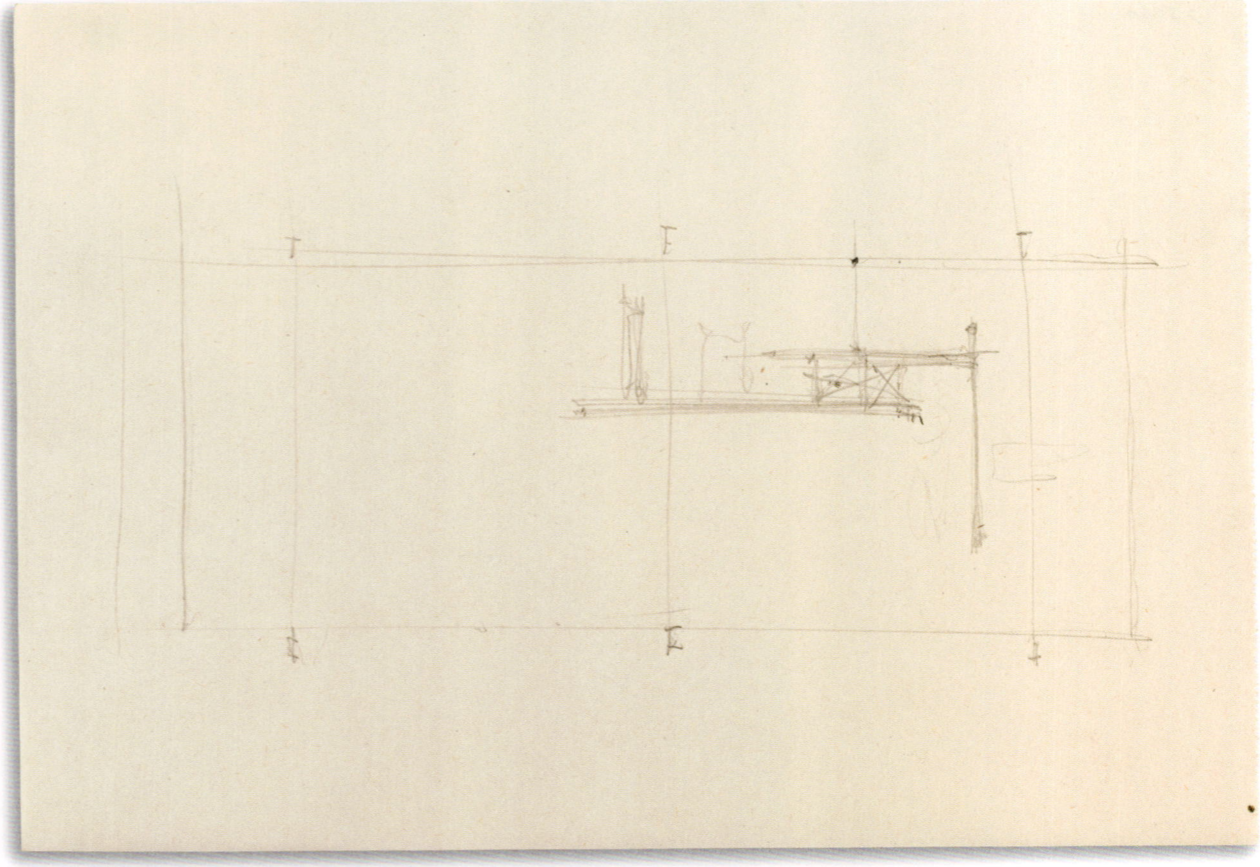

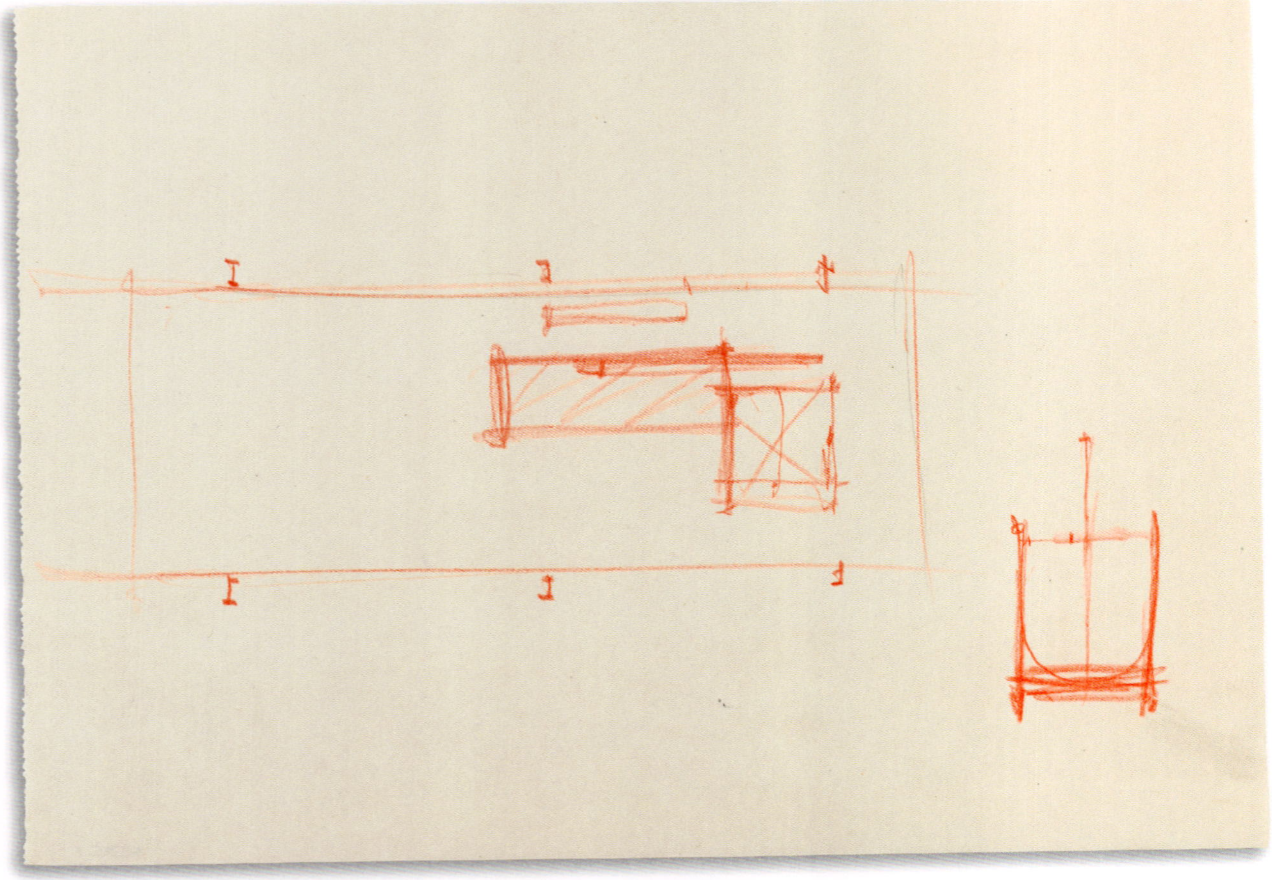

Ludwig Mies van der Rohe, Farnsworth House. Plan, 1945–51.
Colored pencil on notepaper, 6" x 8 1/2" (15.2 cm x 21.6 cm).

Ludwig Mies van der Rohe, Farnsworth House. Aerial perspective, 1945–51.
Colored pencil on notepaper, 6" x 8½" (15.2 cm x 21.6 cm).

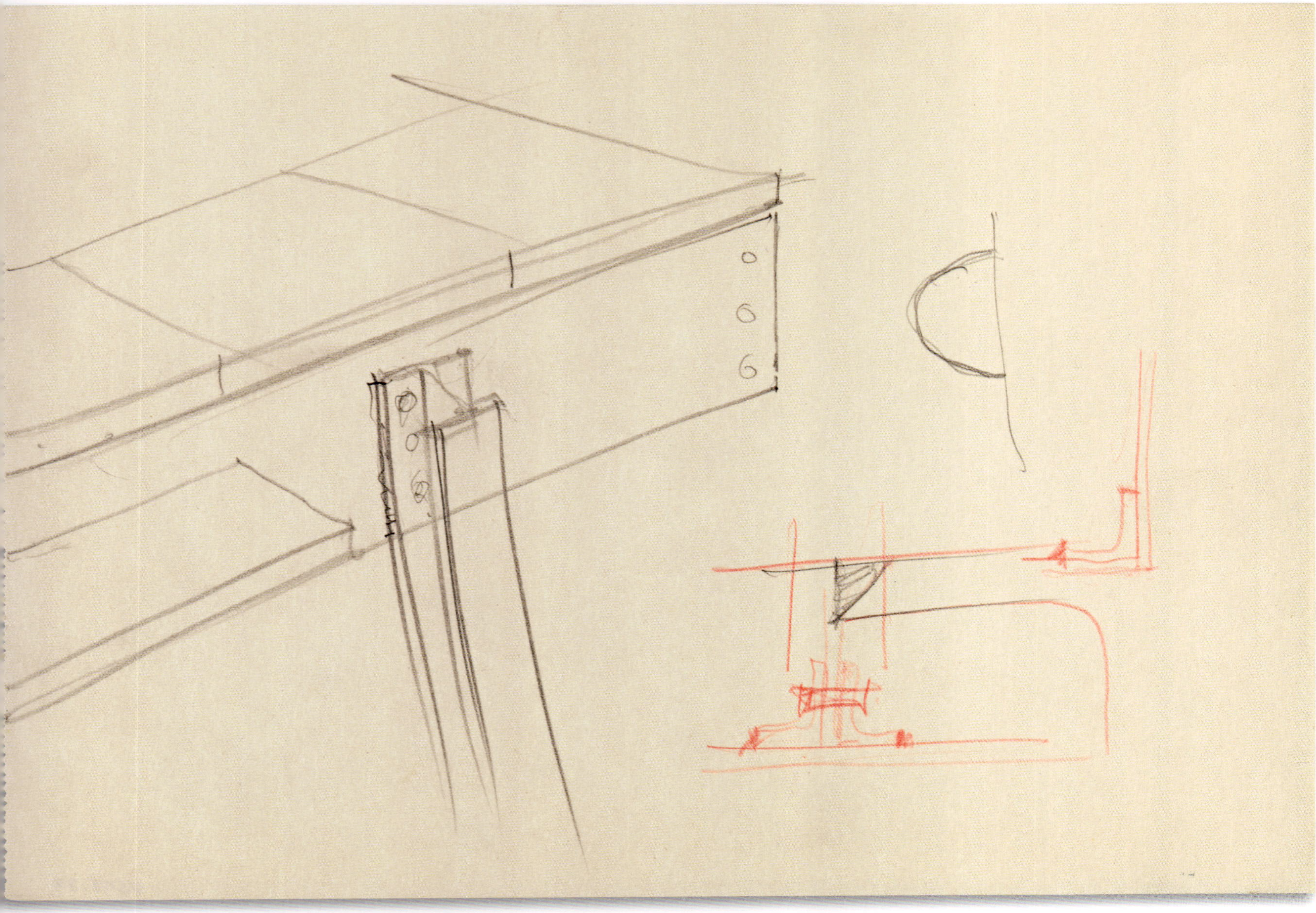

Ludwig Mies van der Rohe, Farnsworth House terrace. Perspective, section, 1945–51.
Pencil and colored pencil on notepaper, 6" x 8 1/2" (15.2 cm x 21.6 cm).

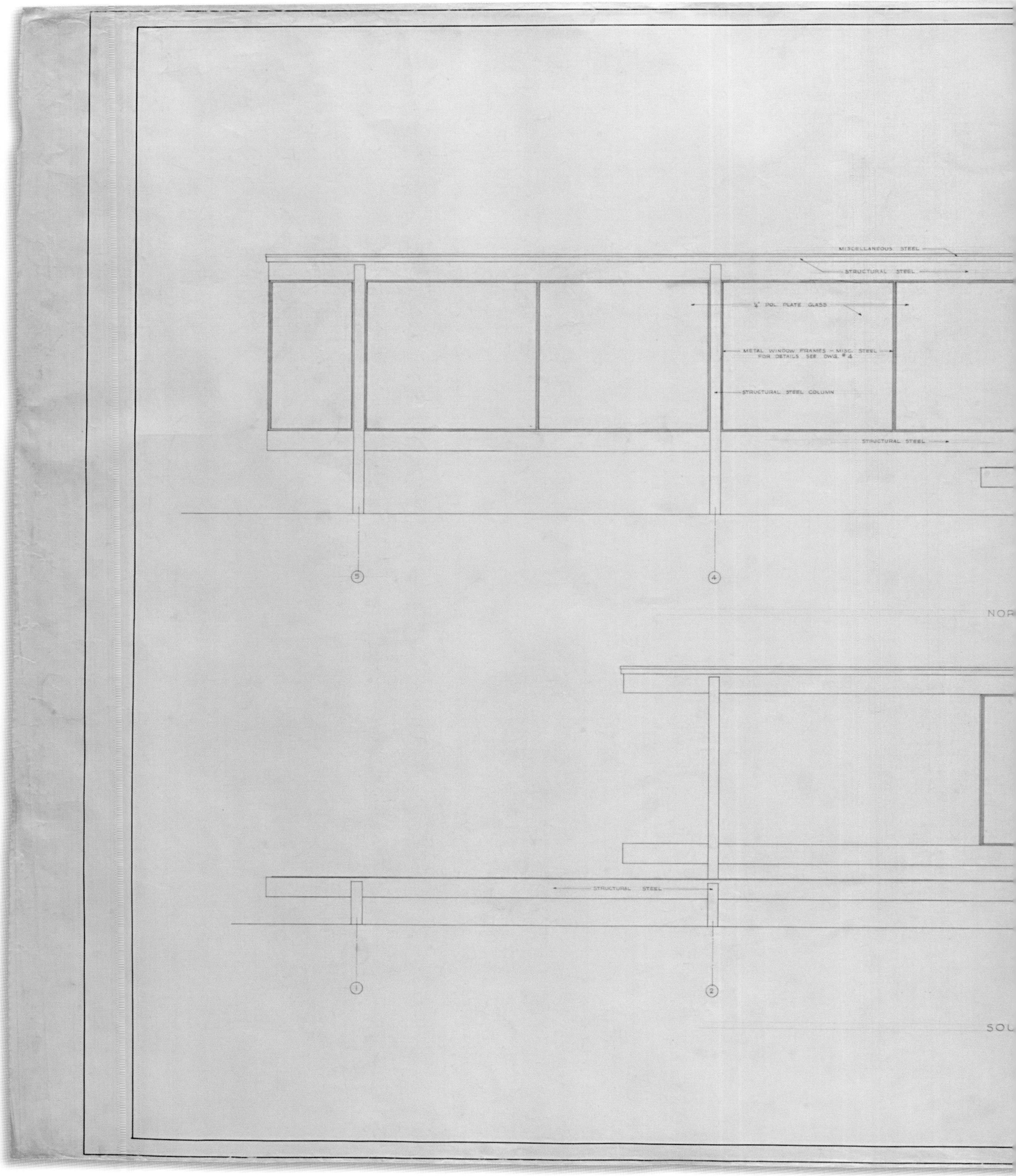

Ludwig Mies van der Rohe, Farnsworth House. Elevations, 1949.
Pencil on ozalid, 37" x 62" (94 cm x 157.5 cm).
© The Museum of Modern Art, New York. The Mies van der Rohe Archive.

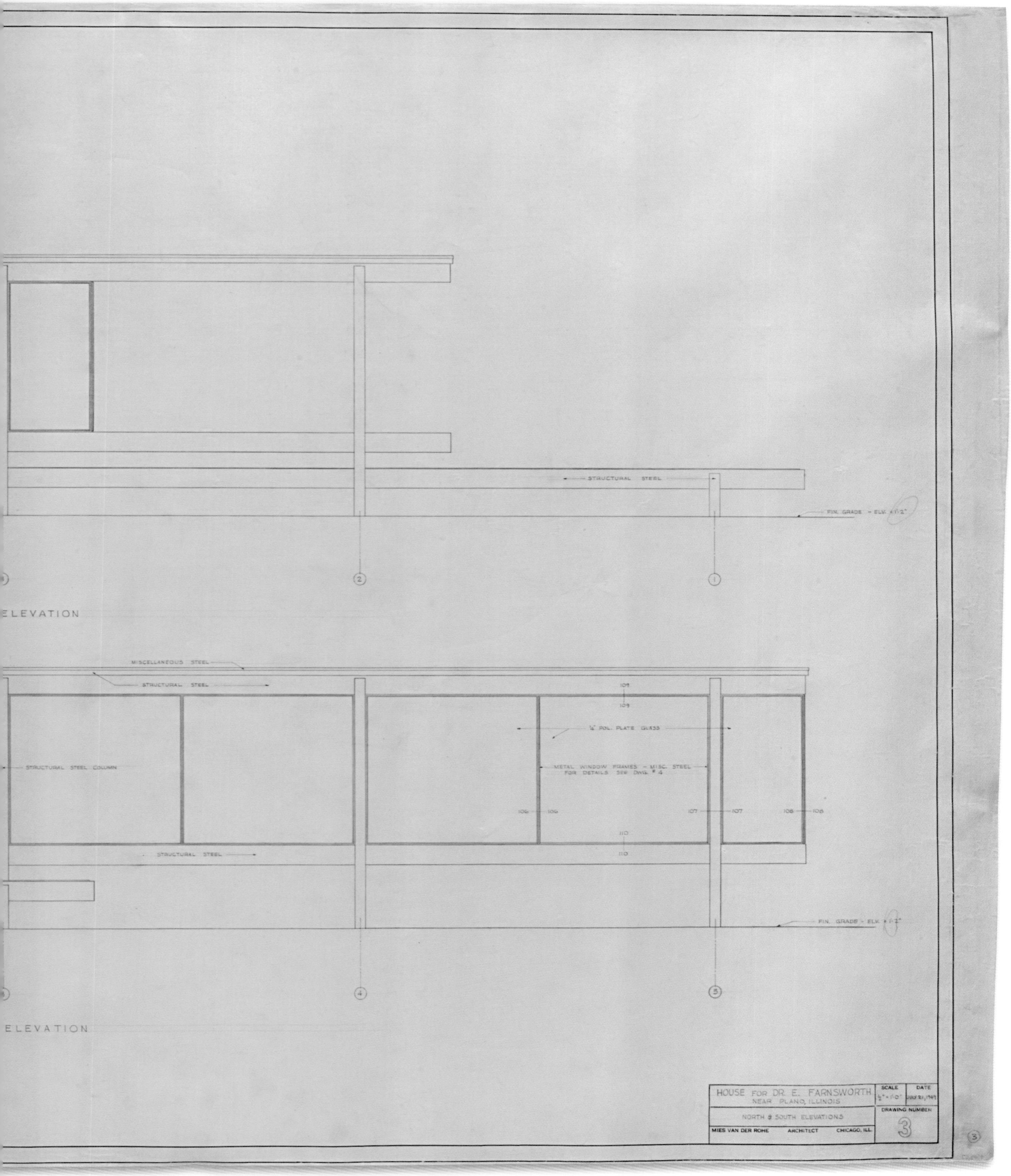
STRUCTURAL STEEL
FIN. GRADE - ELV. +1'-2"
2
1
ELEVATION
MISCELLANEOUS STEEL
STRUCTURAL STEEL
109
109
¼" POL. PLATE GLASS
STRUCTURAL STEEL COLUMN
METAL WINDOW FRAMES - MISC. STEEL
FOR DETAILS SEE DWG. # 4
106
106
107
107
108
108
110
110
STRUCTURAL STEEL
FIN. GRADE - ELV. +1'-2"
4
5
ELEVATION
HOUSE FOR DR. E. FARNSWORTH
NEAR PLANO, ILLINOIS
NORTH & SOUTH ELEVATIONS
MIES VAN DER ROHE ARCHITECT CHICAGO, ILL.
SCALE
½" = 1'-0"
DATE
DRAWING NUMBER
3

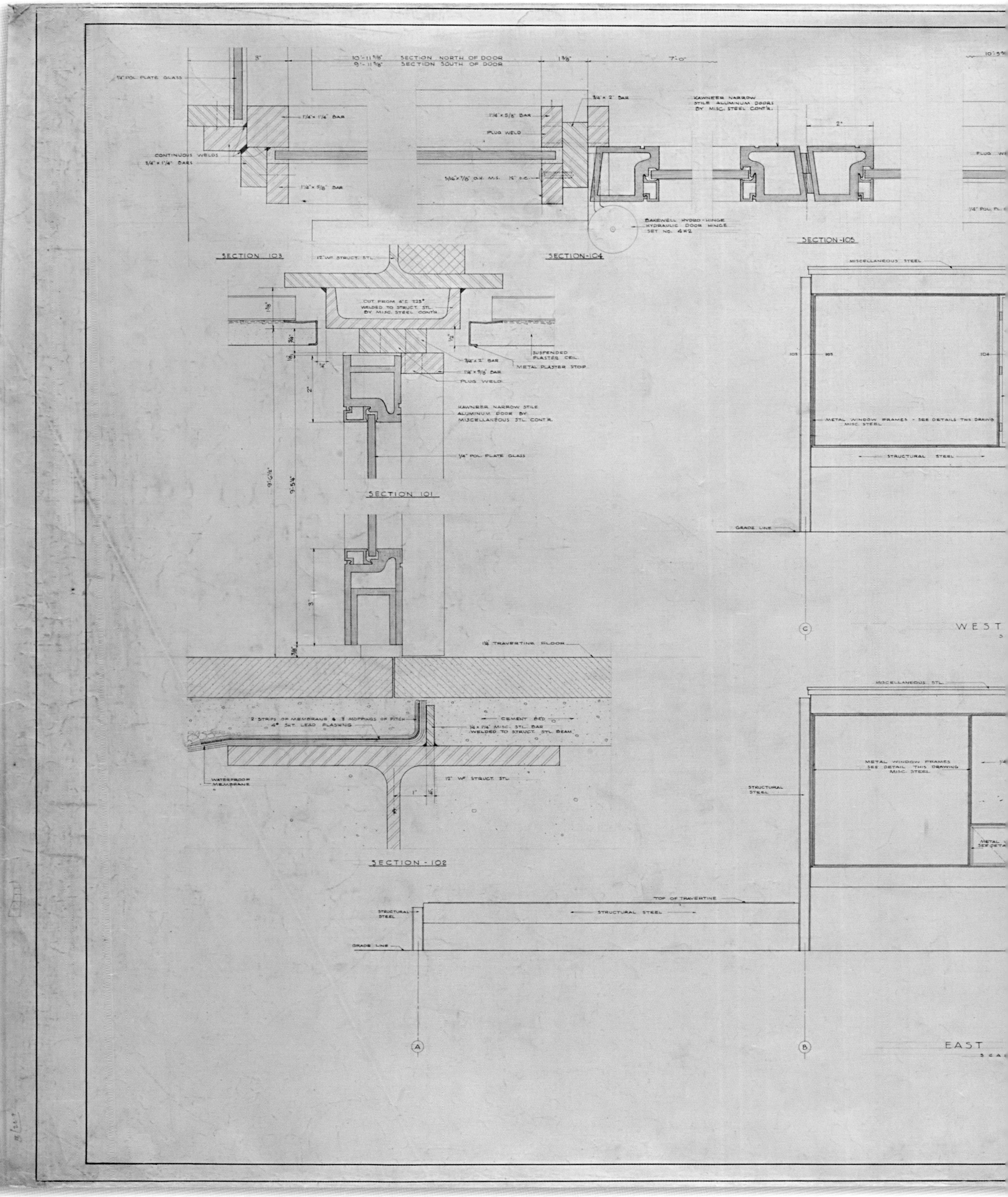

Ludwig Mies van der Rohe, Farnsworth House. Elevations and sections, 1949.
Pencil on ozalid, 37" x 62" (94 cm x 157.5 cm).

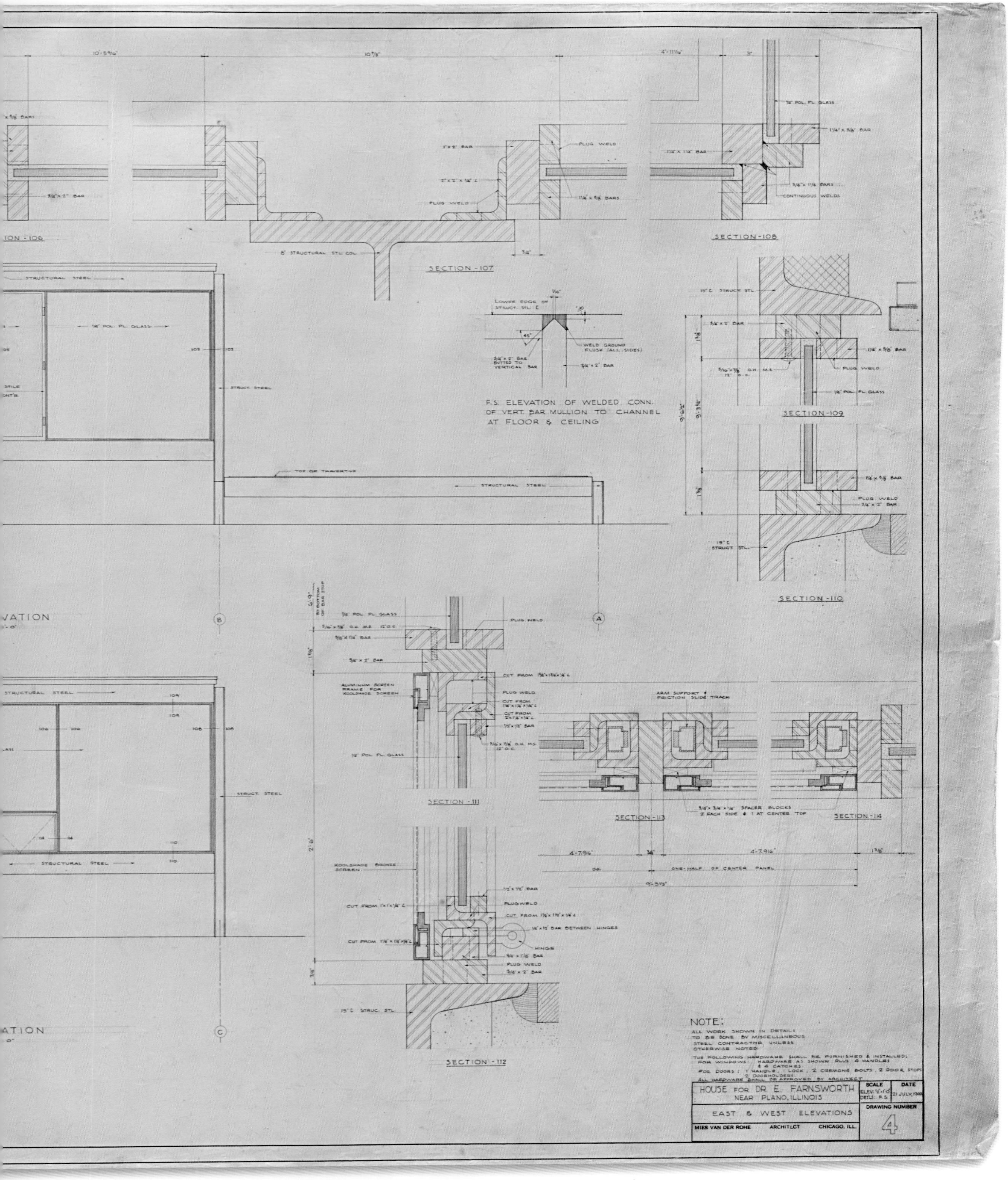
SECTION - 107
SECTION - 108
SECTION - 109
SECTION - 110
SECTION - 111
SECTION - 112
SECTION - 113
SECTION - 114
F.S. ELEVATION OF WELDED CONN. OF VERT. BAR MULLION TO CHANNEL AT FLOOR & CEILING
STRUCTURAL STEEL
1/4" POL. PL. GLASS
STRUCT. STEEL
TOP OF TRAVERTINE
PLUG WELD
HINGE
NOTE:
ALL WORK SHOWN IN DETAILS TO BE DONE BY MISCELLANEOUS STEEL CONTRACTOR UNLESS OTHERWISE NOTED.
THE FOLLOWING HARDWARE SHALL BE FURNISHED & INSTALLED;
FOR WINDOWS: HARDWARE AS SHOWN PLUS 4 HANDLES & 4 CATCHES.
FOR DOORS: 1 HANDLE, 1 LOCK, 2 CREMONE BOLTS, 2 DOOR STOPS, 2 DOORHOLDERS.
ALL HARDWARE SHALL BE APPROVED BY ARCHITECT
HOUSE FOR DR. E. FARNSWORTH
NEAR PLANO, ILLINOIS
SCALE
DATE
21 JULY, 1949
EAST & WEST ELEVATIONS
DRAWING NUMBER
4
MIES VAN DER ROHE
ARCHITECT
CHICAGO, ILL.

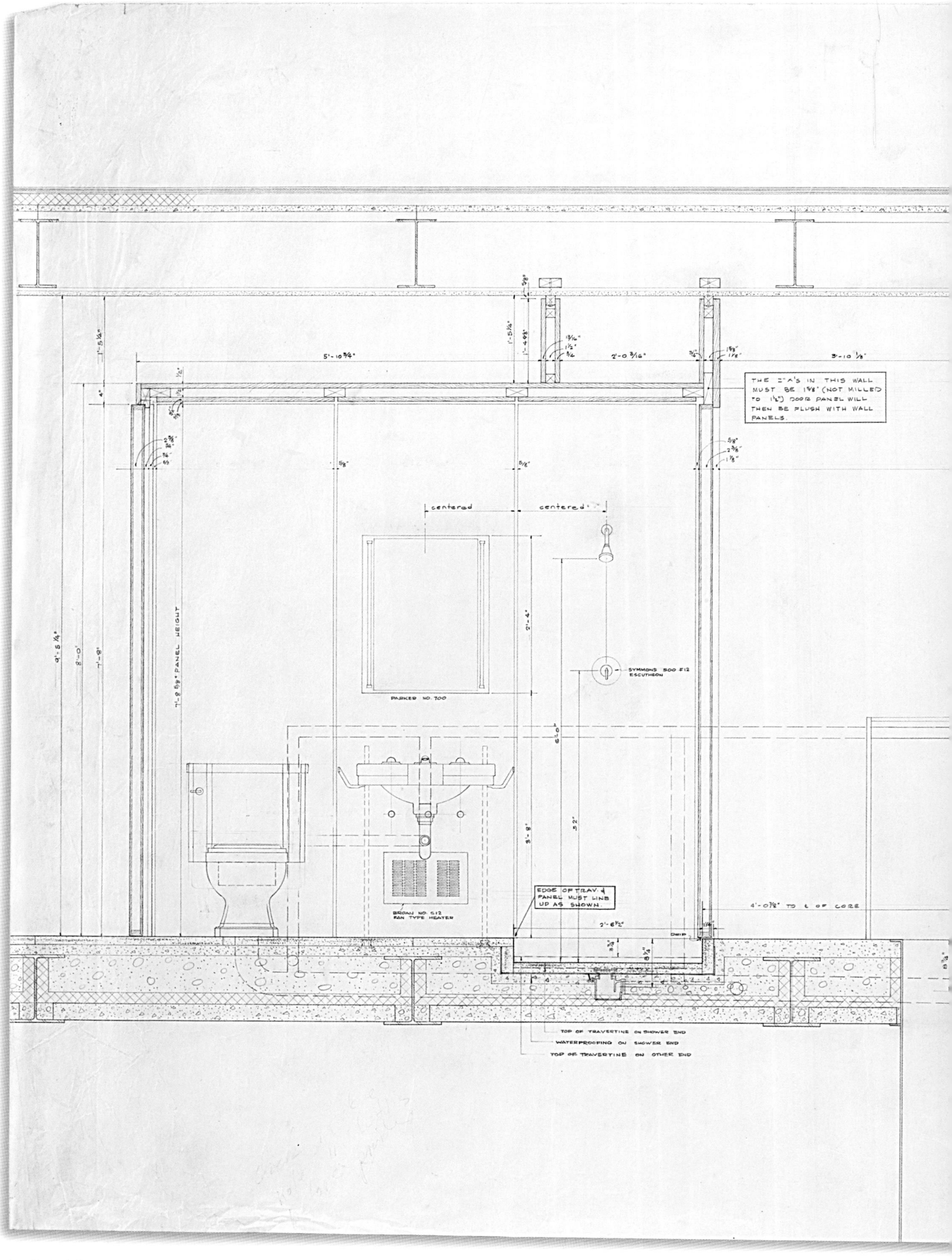

Ludwig Mies van der Rohe, Farnsworth House. Section through core, 1949.
Pencil on ozalid, 27" x 42" (68.6 cm x 106.7 cm).

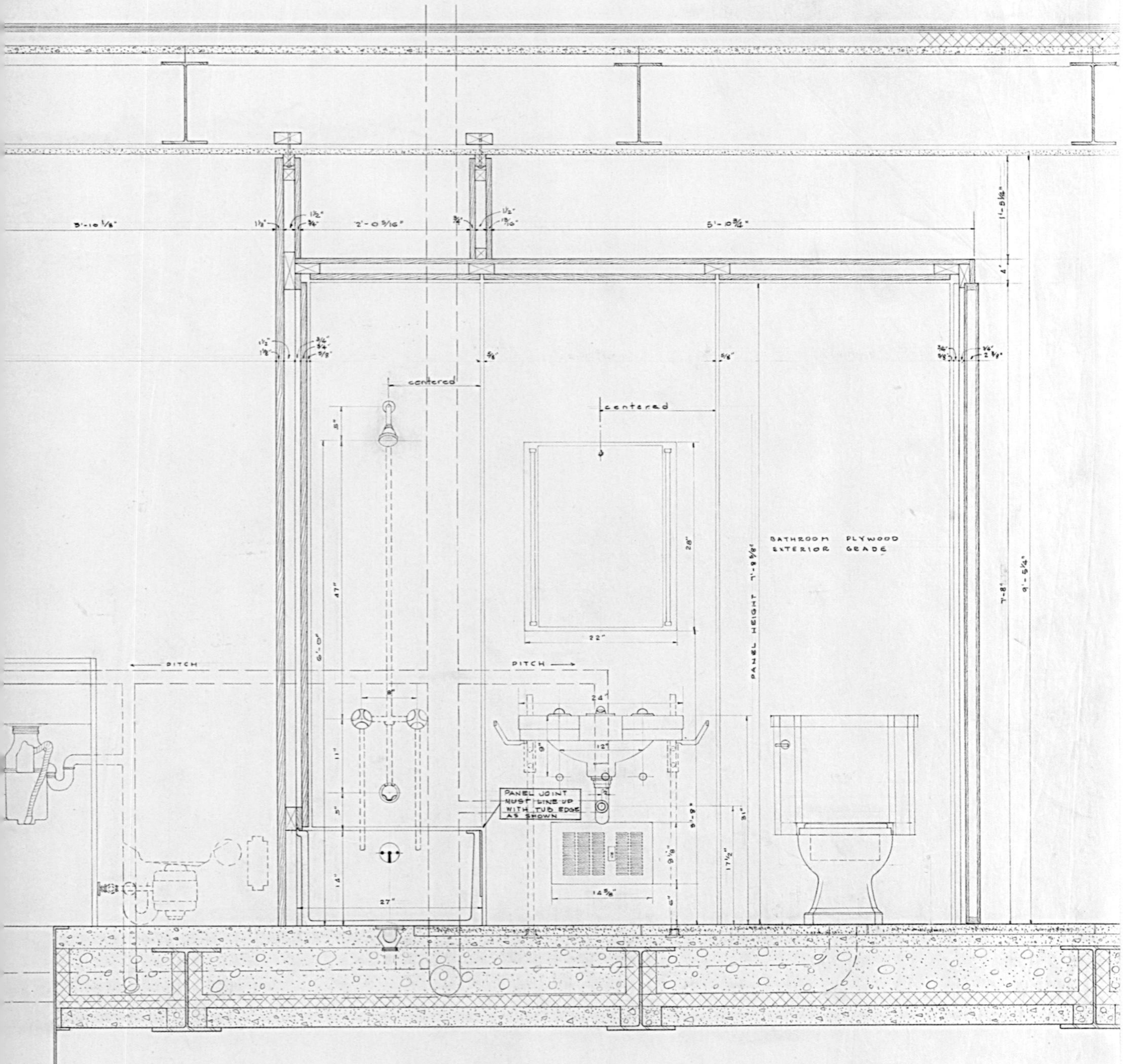

SECTION THRU CORE
FARNSWORTH HOUSE
1½" = 1'-0"

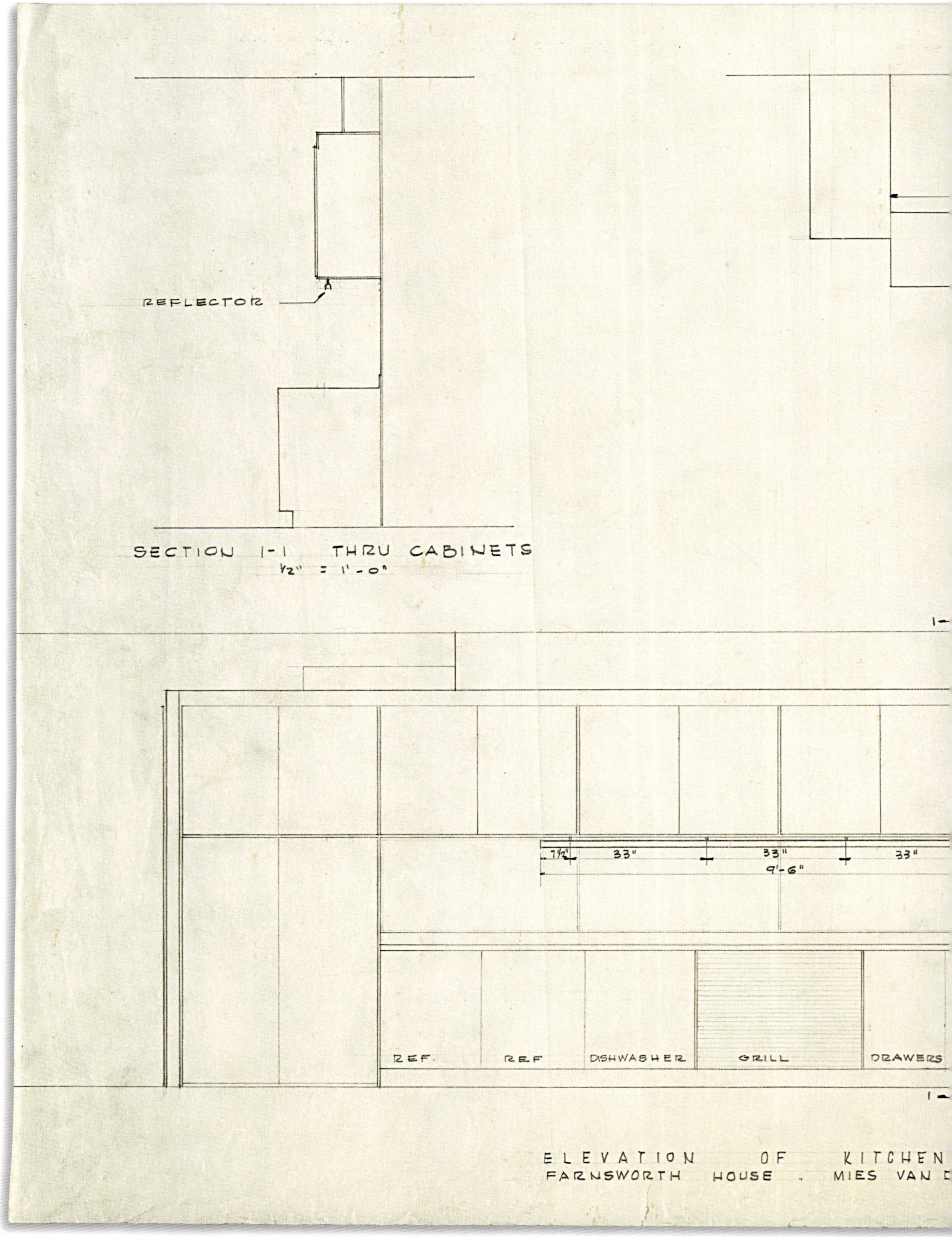

Ludwig Mies van der Rohe, Farnsworth House. Elevation of kitchen and sections, 1950.
Pencil on vellum, 12 1/2" x 19" (31.8 cm x 48.3 cm).
© The Museum of Modern Art, New York. The Mies van der Rohe Archive.

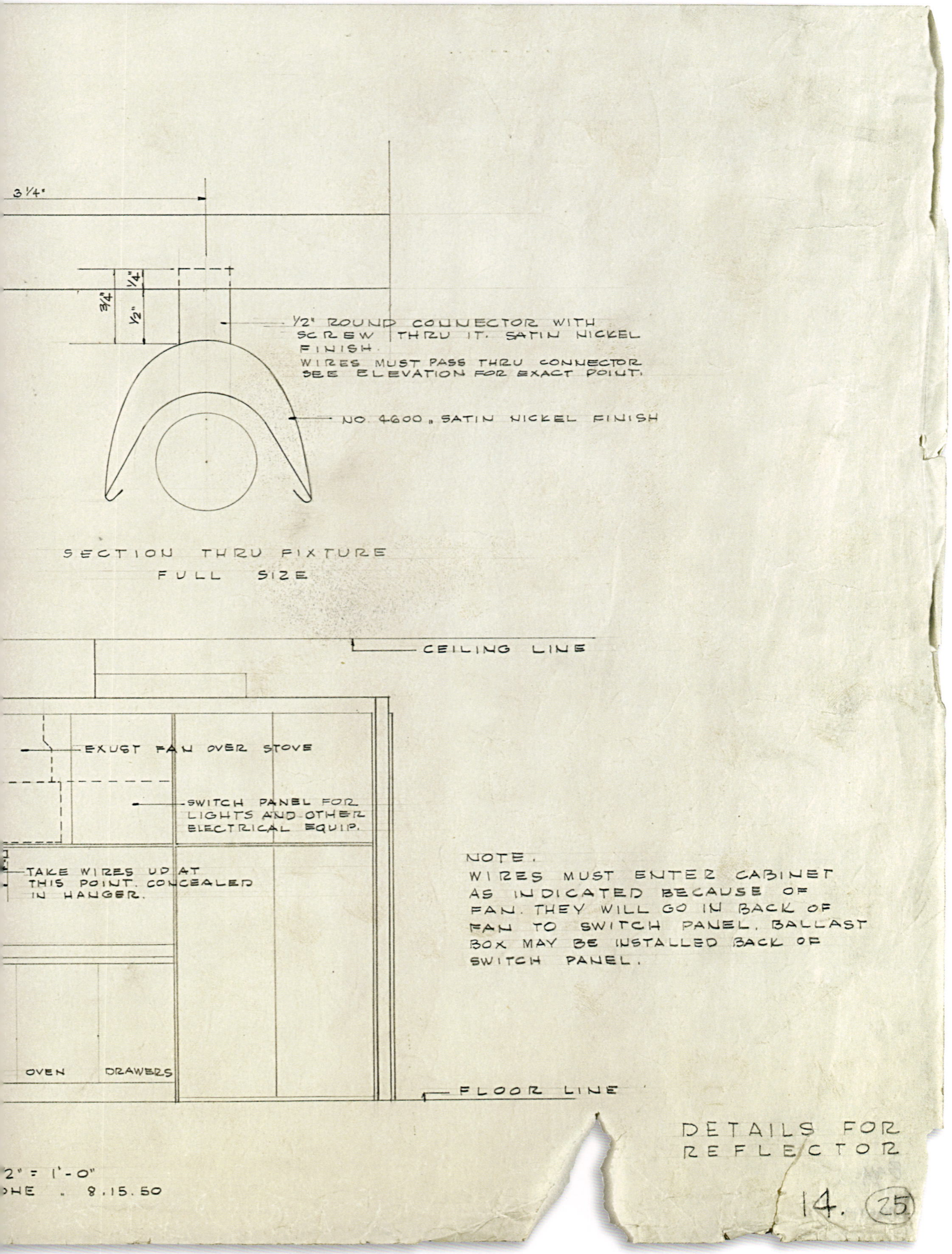
3 1/4"
3/4"
1/4"
1/2"
1/2" ROUND CONNECTOR WITH SCREW THRU IT. SATIN NICKEL FINISH.
WIRES MUST PASS THRU CONNECTOR SEE ELEVATION FOR EXACT POINT.
NO. 4600 " SATIN NICKEL FINISH
SECTION THRU FIXTURE
FULL SIZE
CEILING LINE
EXUST FAN OVER STOVE
SWITCH PANEL FOR LIGHTS AND OTHER ELECTRICAL EQUIP.
TAKE WIRES UP AT THIS POINT. CONCEALED IN HANGER.
NOTE.
WIRES MUST ENTER CABINET AS INDICATED BECAUSE OF FAN. THEY WILL GO IN BACK OF FAN TO SWITCH PANEL, BALLAST BOX MAY BE INSTALLED BACK OF SWITCH PANEL.
OVEN
DRAWERS
FLOOR LINE
DETAILS FOR REFLECTOR
2" = 1'-0"
DHE . 8.15.50
14. 25

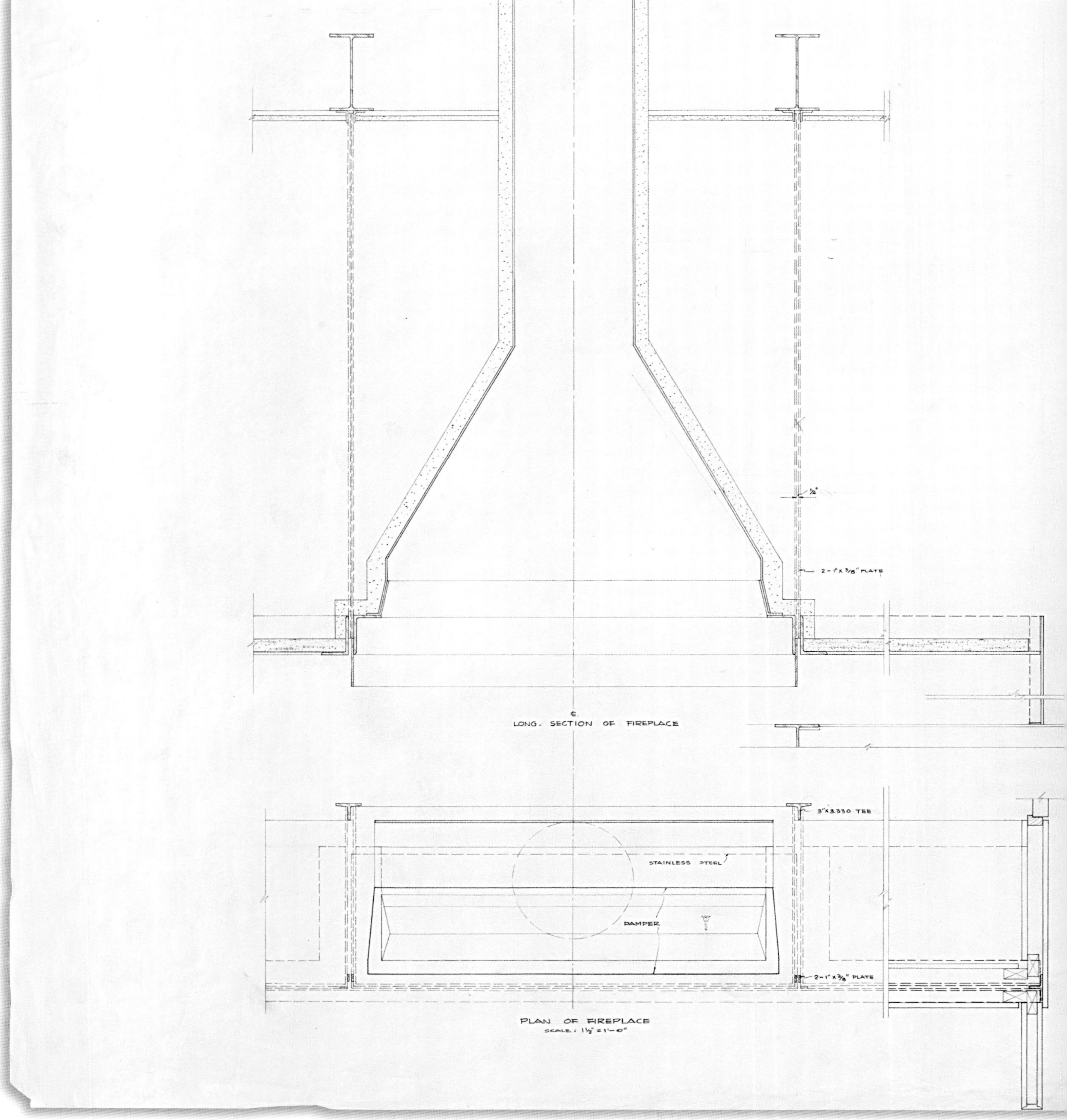

Ludwig Mies van der Rohe, Farnsworth House. Plan, cross section, and section of fireplace, 1949–51.
Pencil on vellum, 31" x 42" (78.7 cm x 106.7 cm).

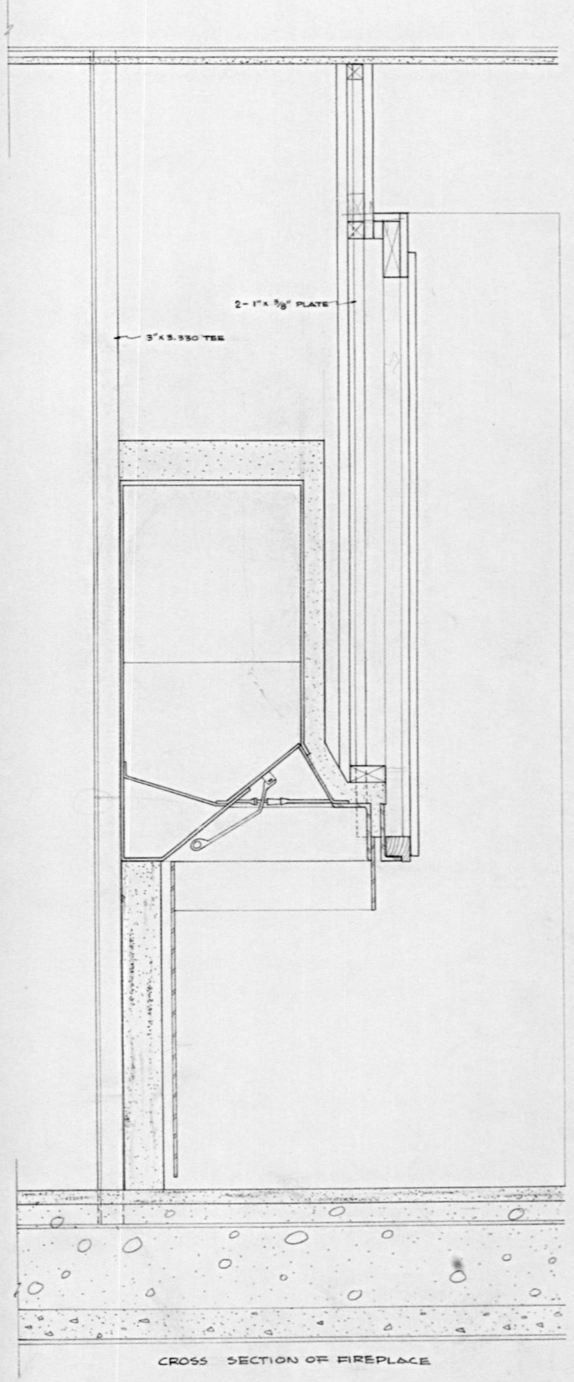

CROSS SECTION OF FIREPLACE

Ludwig Mies van der Rohe, Farnsworth House roof. Section, 1949–51. Pencil on paper, 21" x 36" (53.3 cm x 91.4 cm).

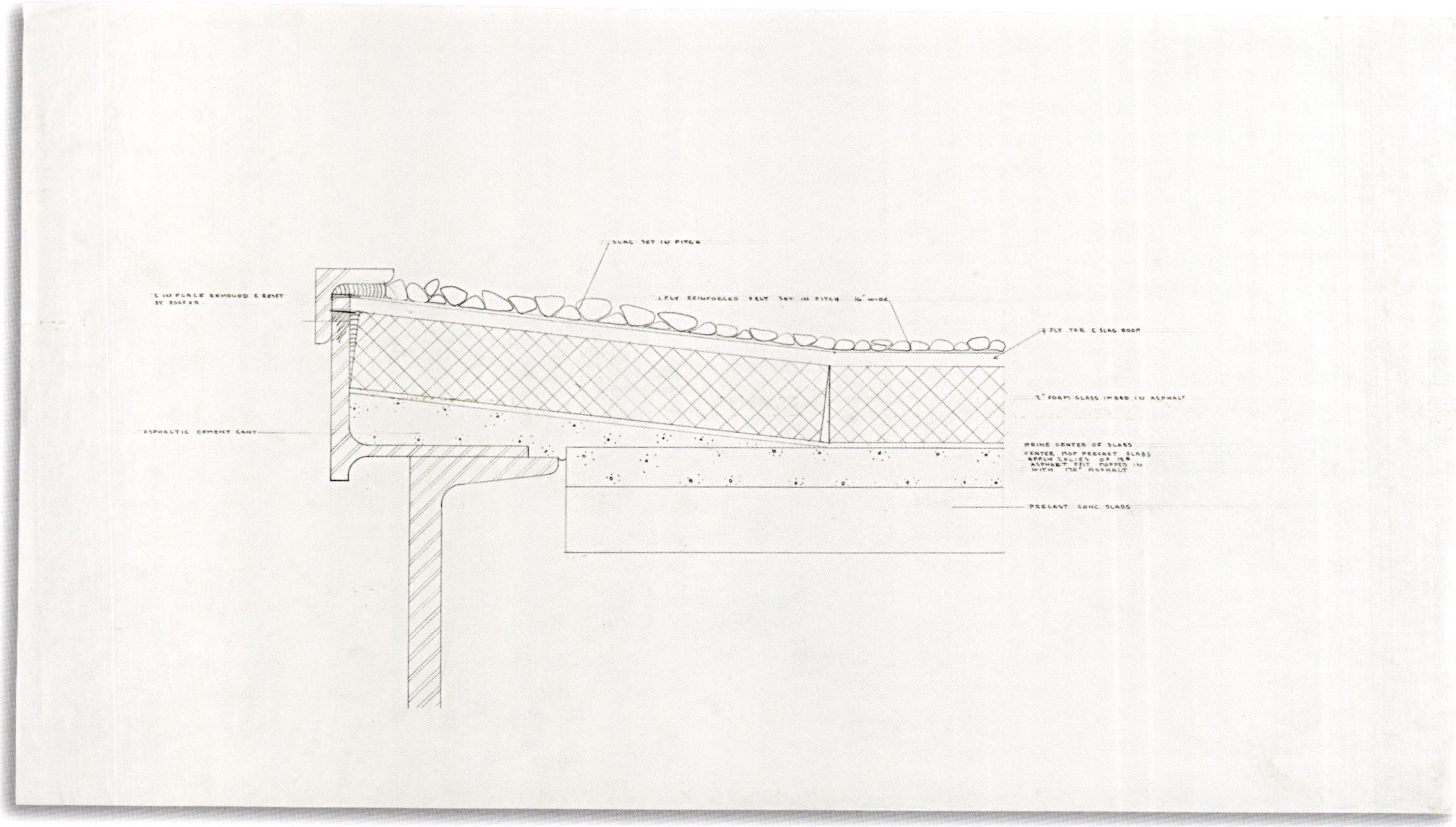

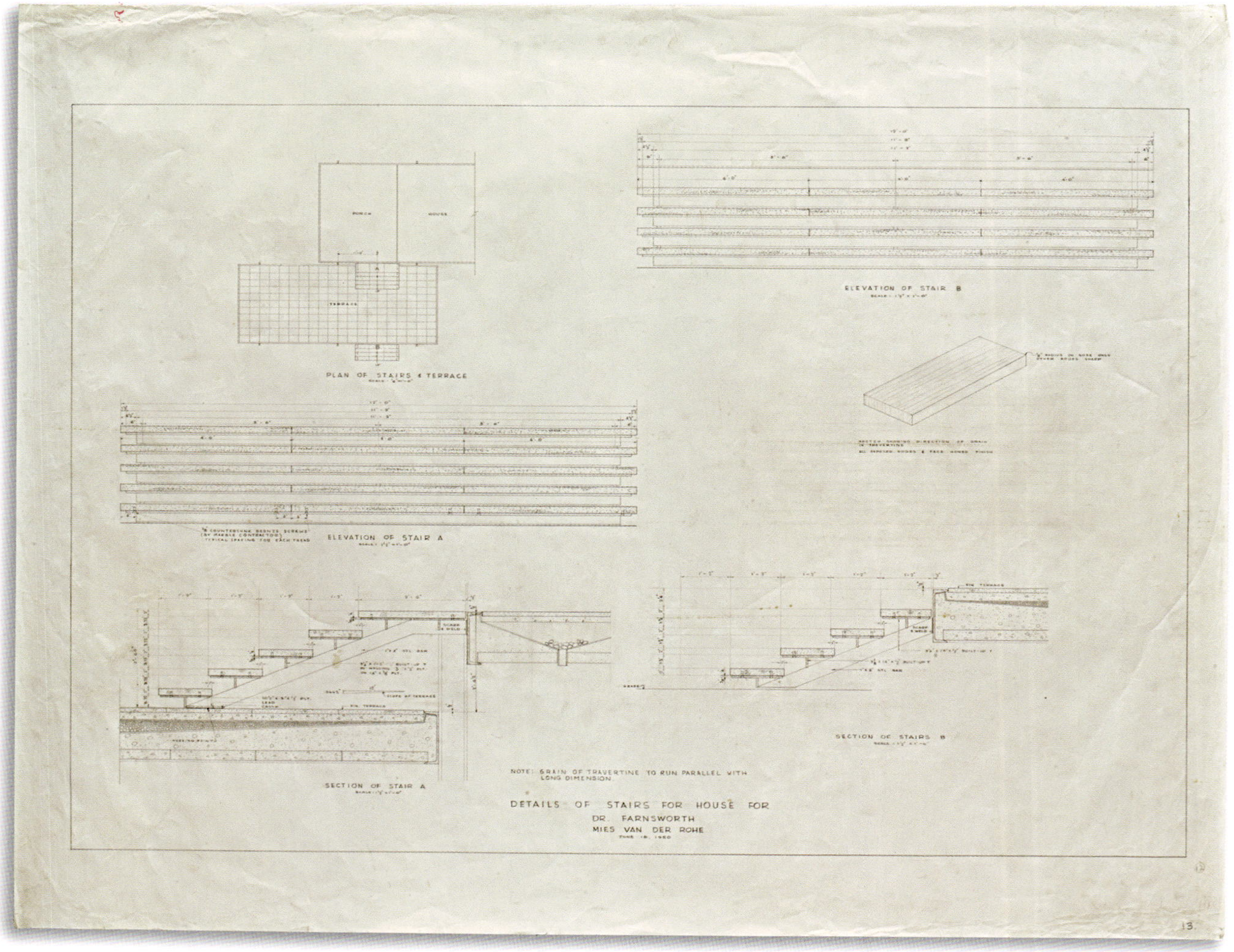

Ludwig Mies van der Rohe, Farnsworth House. Details of stairs, 1950.
Pencil on vellum, 33" x 42" (83.8 cm x 106.7 cm).

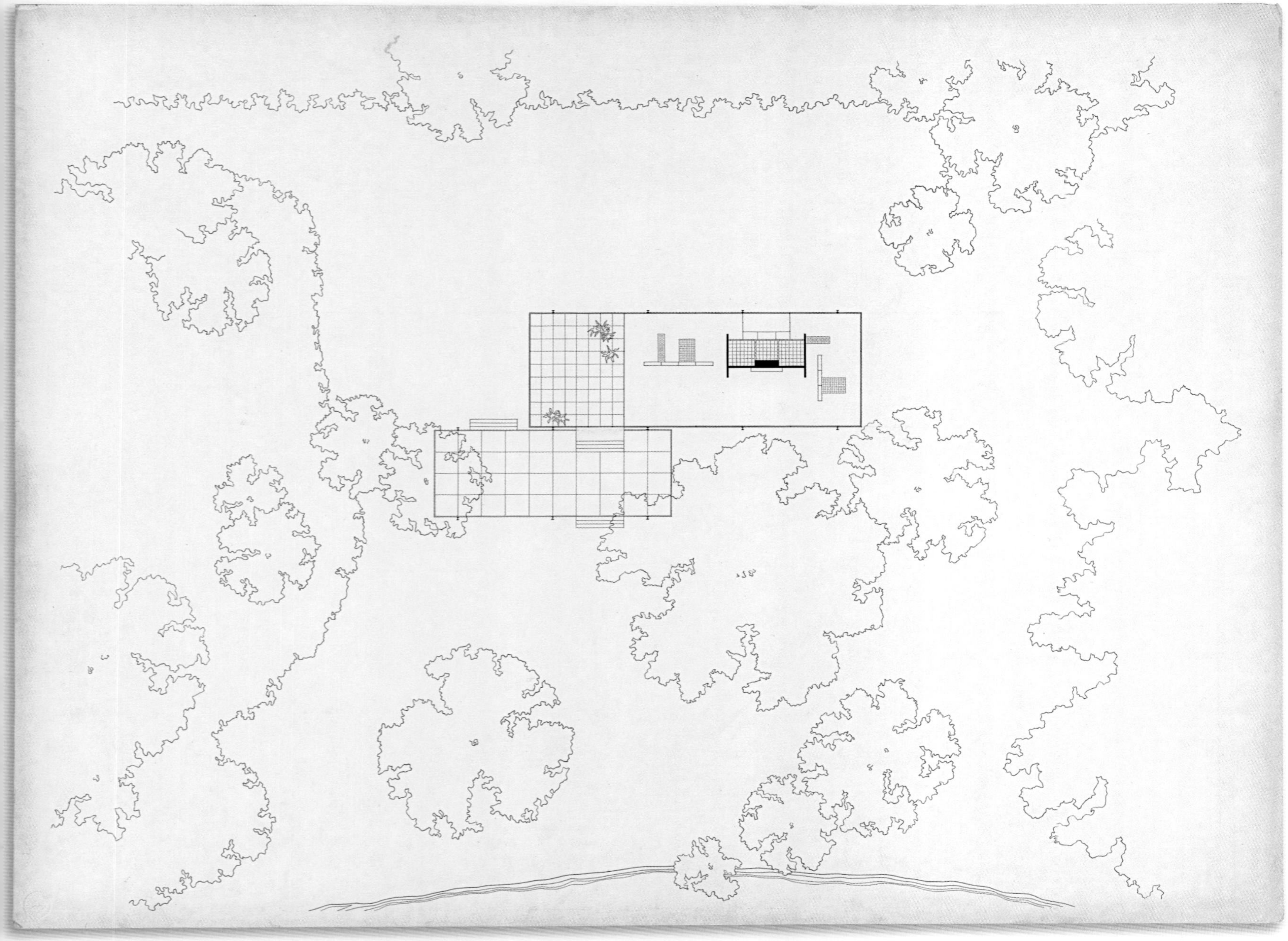

Ludwig Mies van der Rohe, Farnsworth House. Preliminary version: plan, 1945–51.
Ink on paper, 30" x 40" (76.2 cm x 101.6 cm).

Philip Johnson, three buildings connected by pergolas, Scheme IV, plan, first version, 1946.

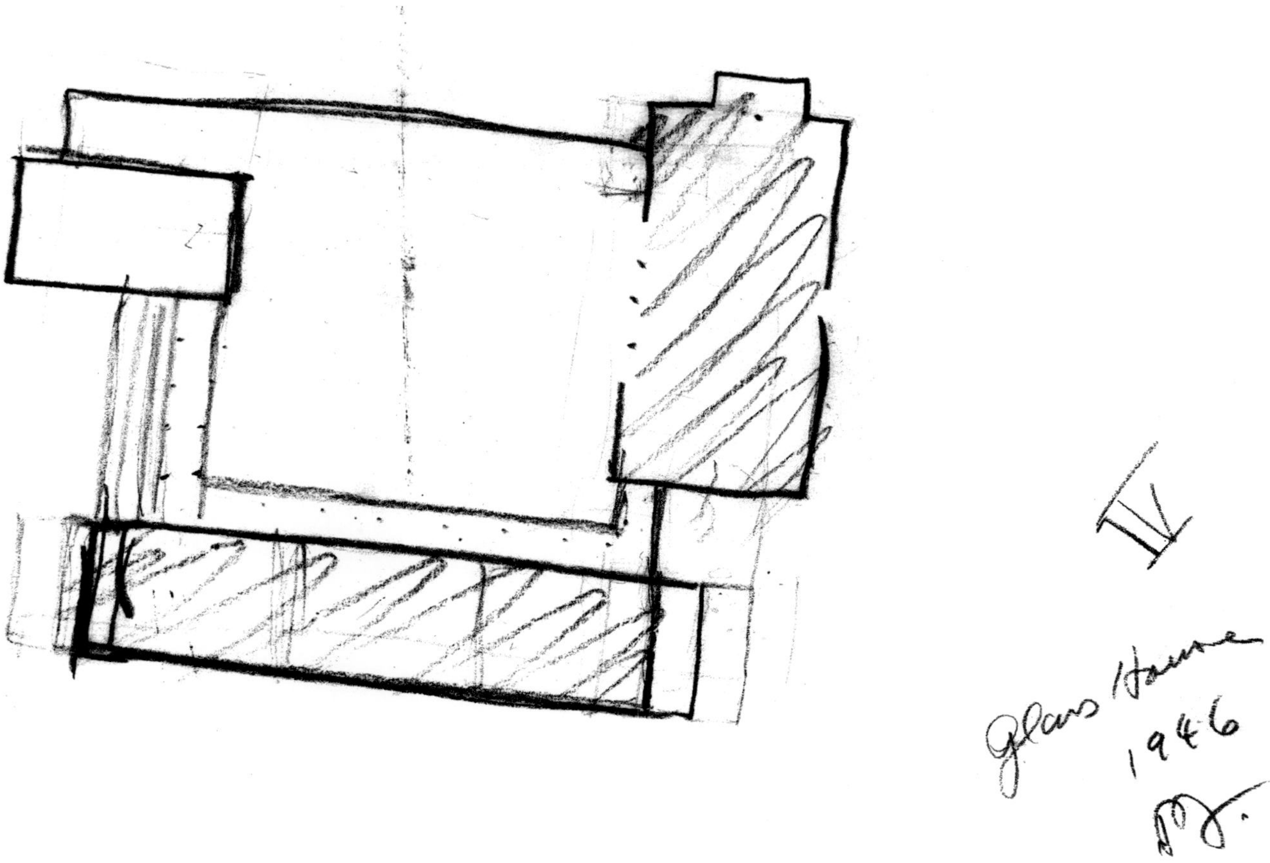

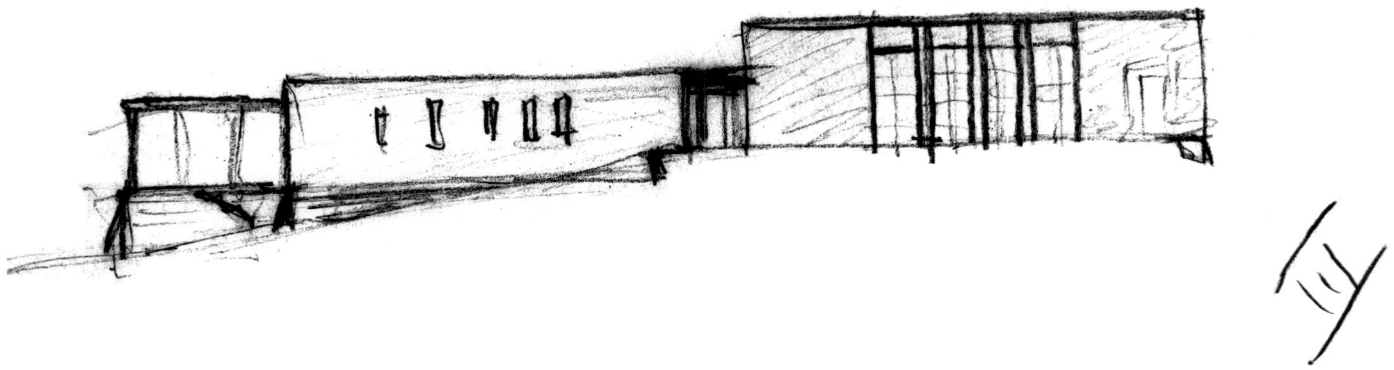

Philip Johnson, three buildings connected by pergolas, Scheme III, east elevation, 1946.

6. PLANS
The Glass House

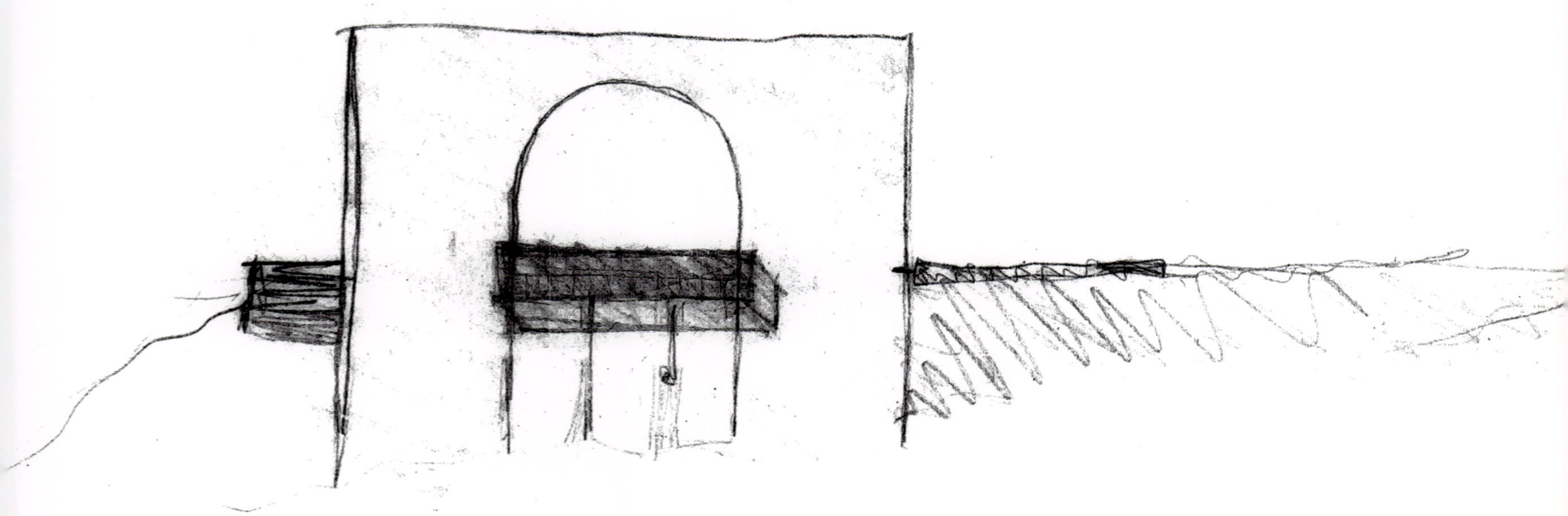

Philip Johnson, house with arches, Scheme XX, south facade, 1947.
All drawings, unless otherwise indicated, are courtesy of the Architectural Drawing Archive, Philip Johnson Glass House, National Trust for Historic Preservation.

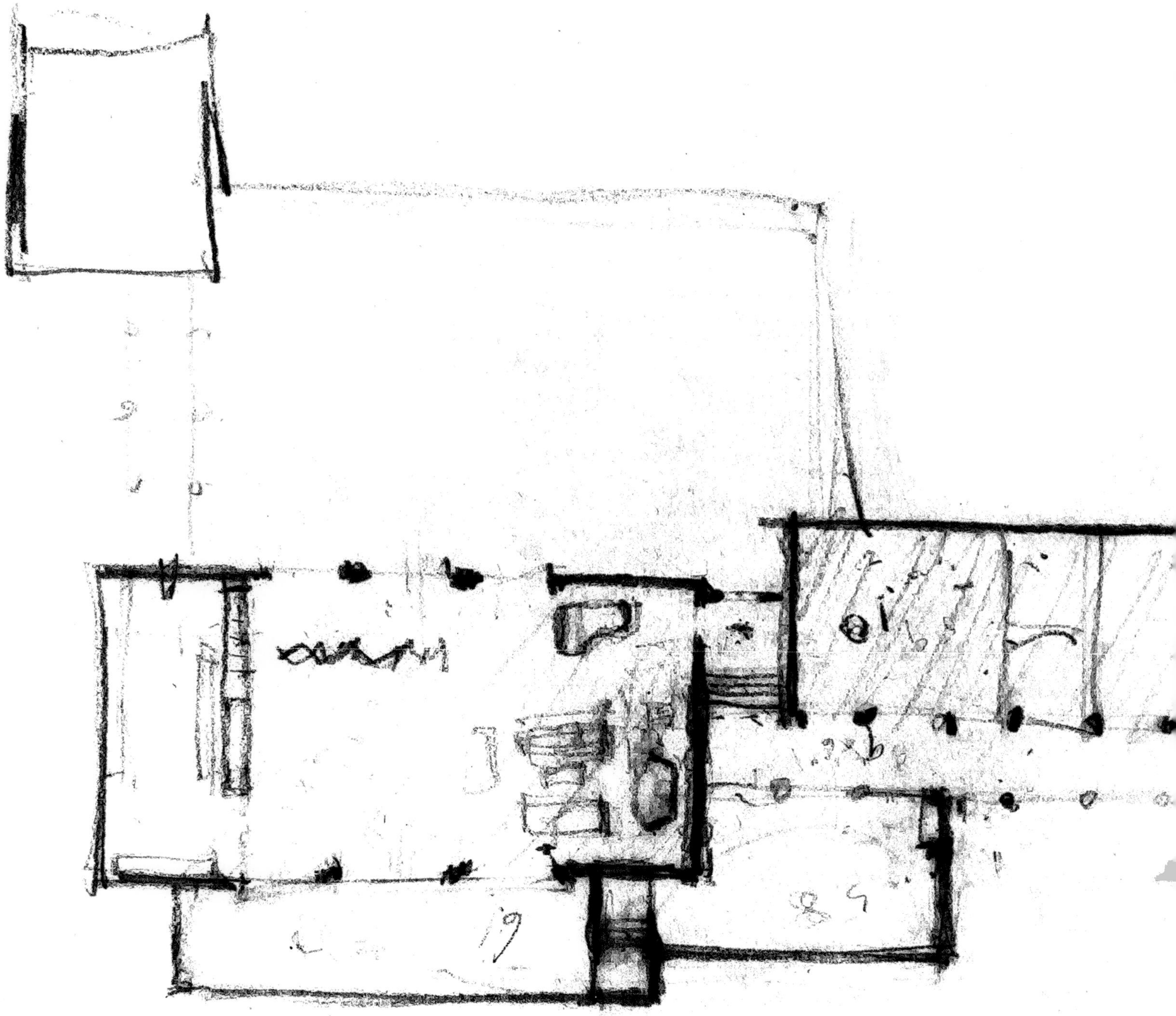

Philip Johnson, three buildings connected by pergolas, Scheme III, plan, 1946.

Philip Johnson, house with arches, Scheme XXI, east elevation, 1947.

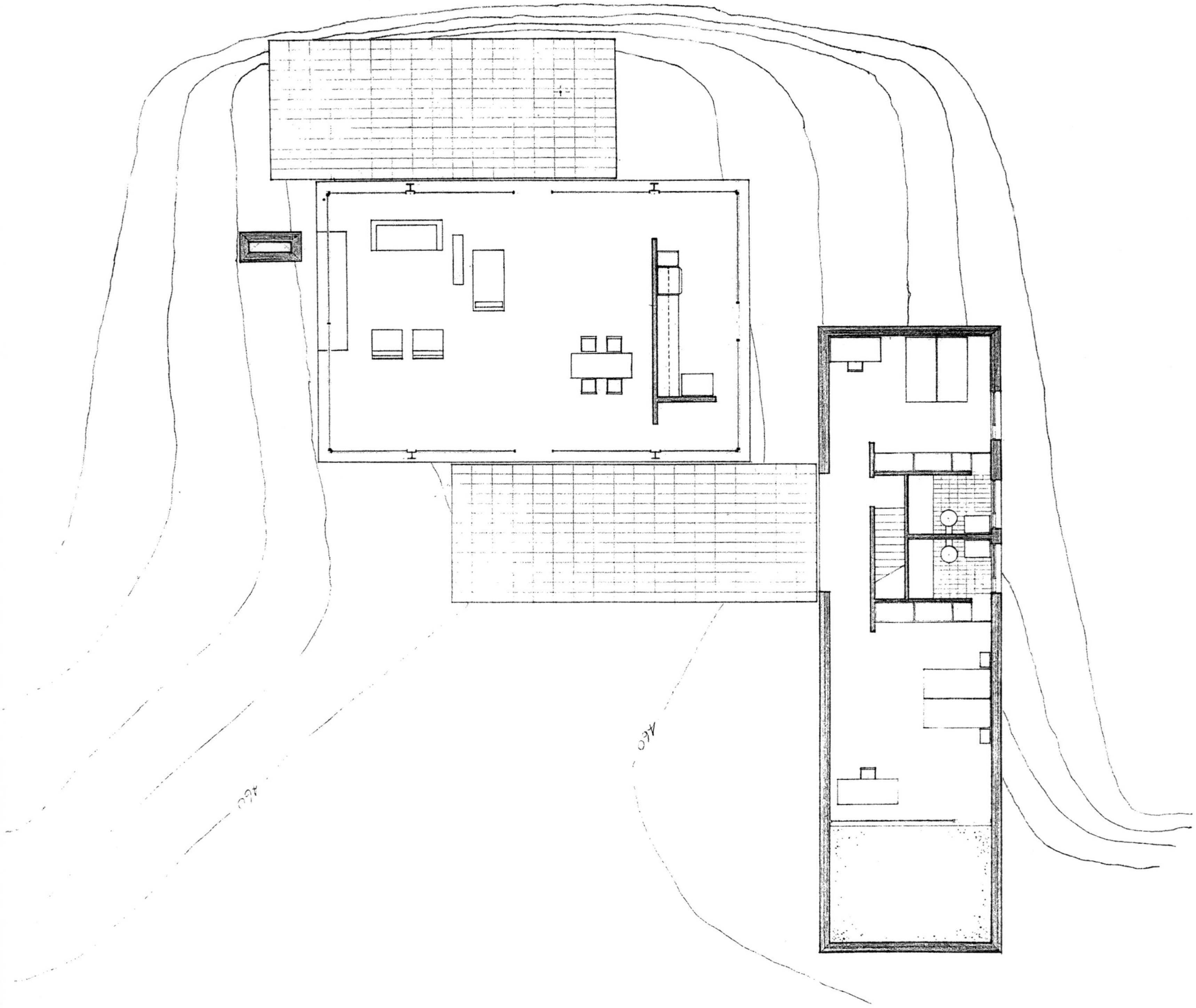

Philip Johnson, Glass House and guesthouse linked by a terrace, Scheme XVI, 1947.

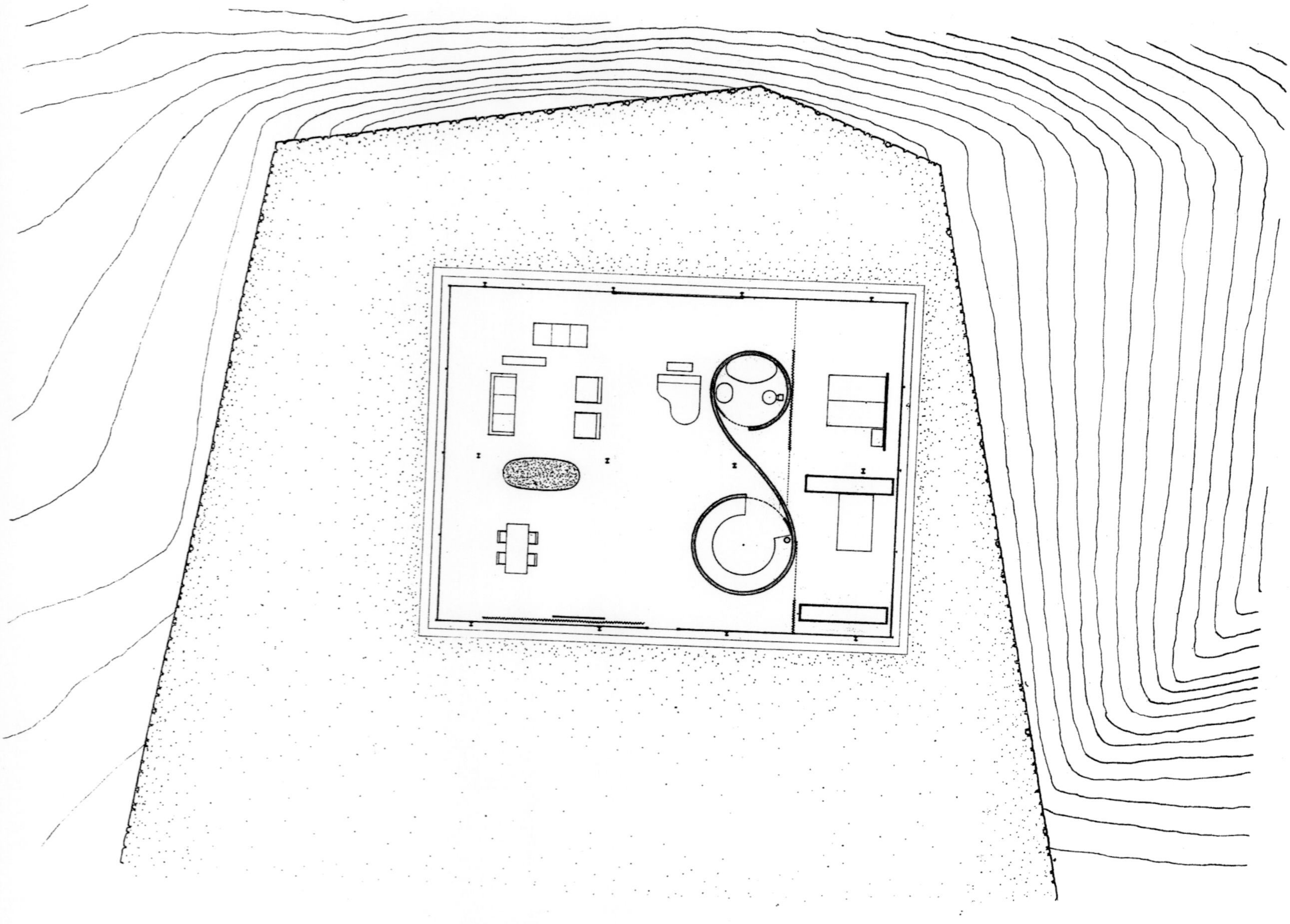

Philip Johnson, house with spiral core, Scheme X, plan, 1946.

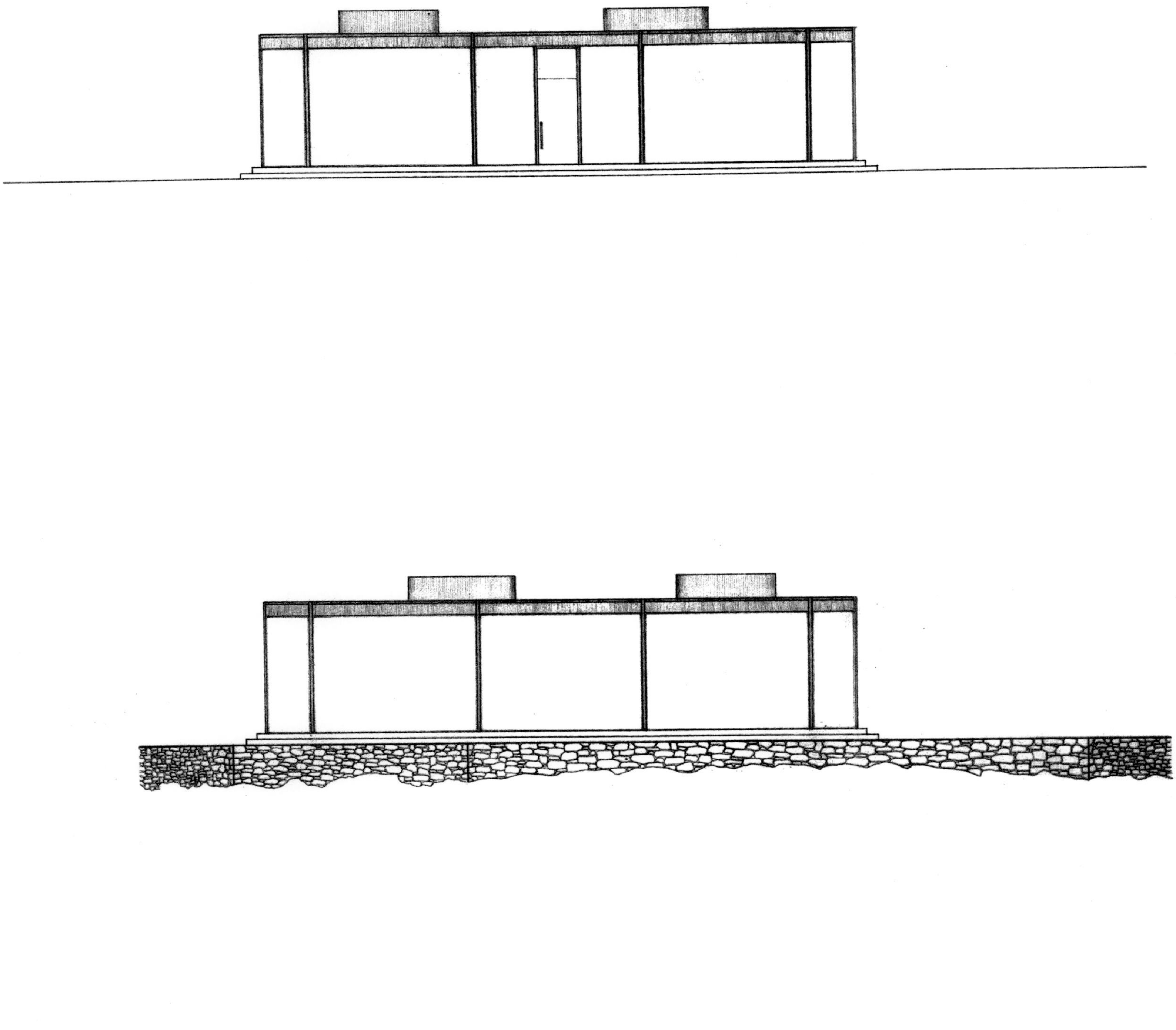

Philip Johnson, house with spiral core, Scheme X, east (top) and west (bottom) elevations, 1946.

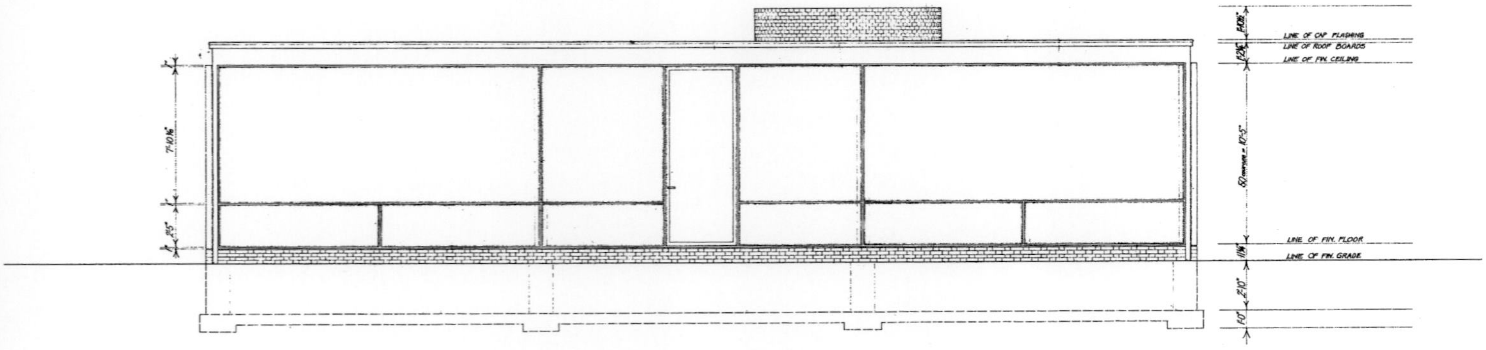

EAST ELEVATION
WEST SIMILAR

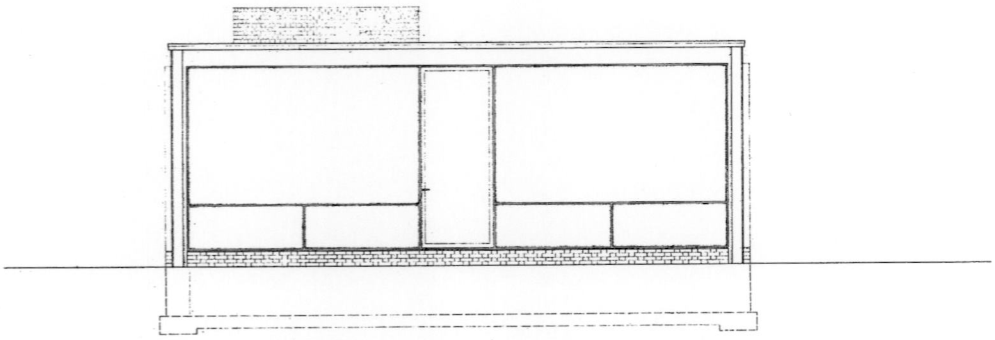

NORTH ELEVATION
SOUTH SIMILAR

Philip Johnson, Glass House, final elevations, 1948.

Philip Johnson, Brick House (unbuilt), plan and three elevations, 1947.

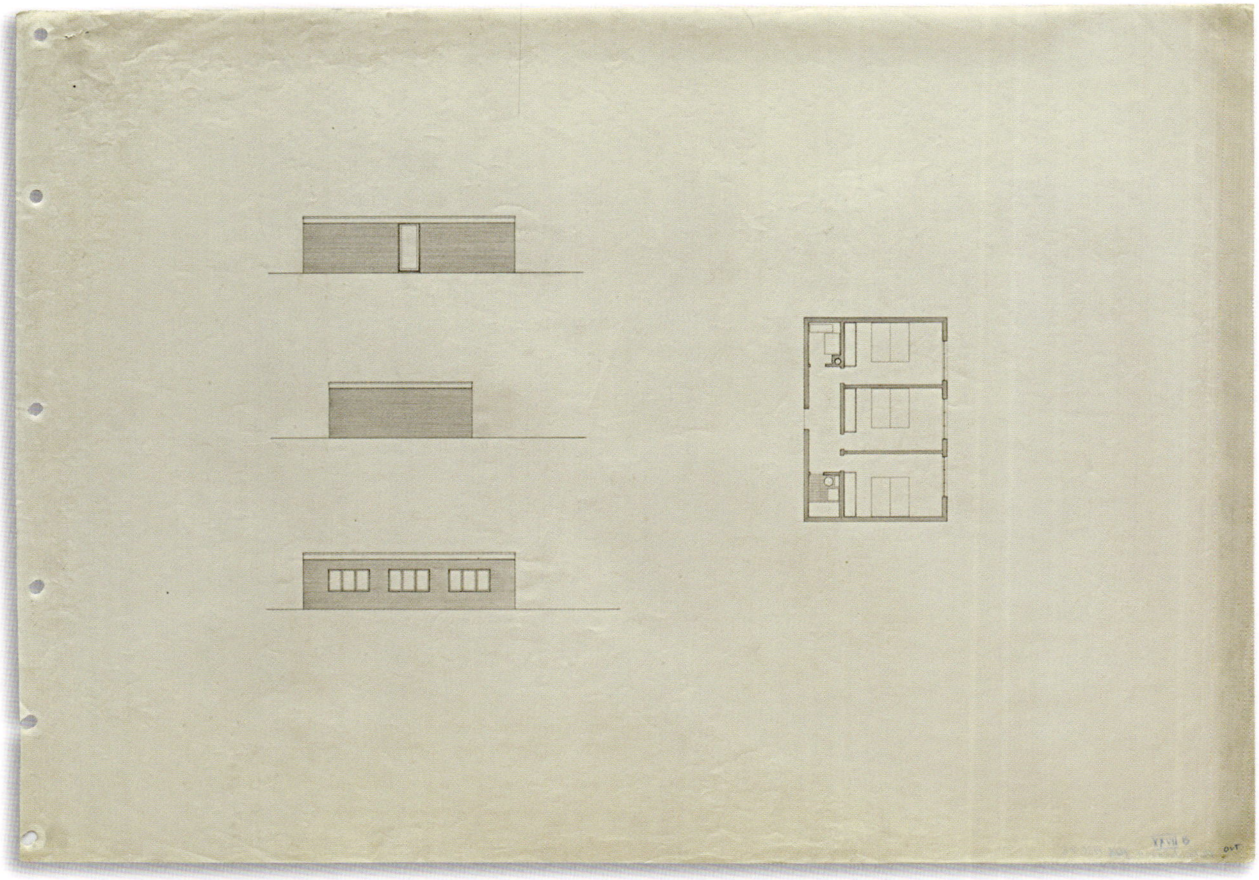

Philip Johnson, Brick House (unbuilt), plan and two elevations, 1947.

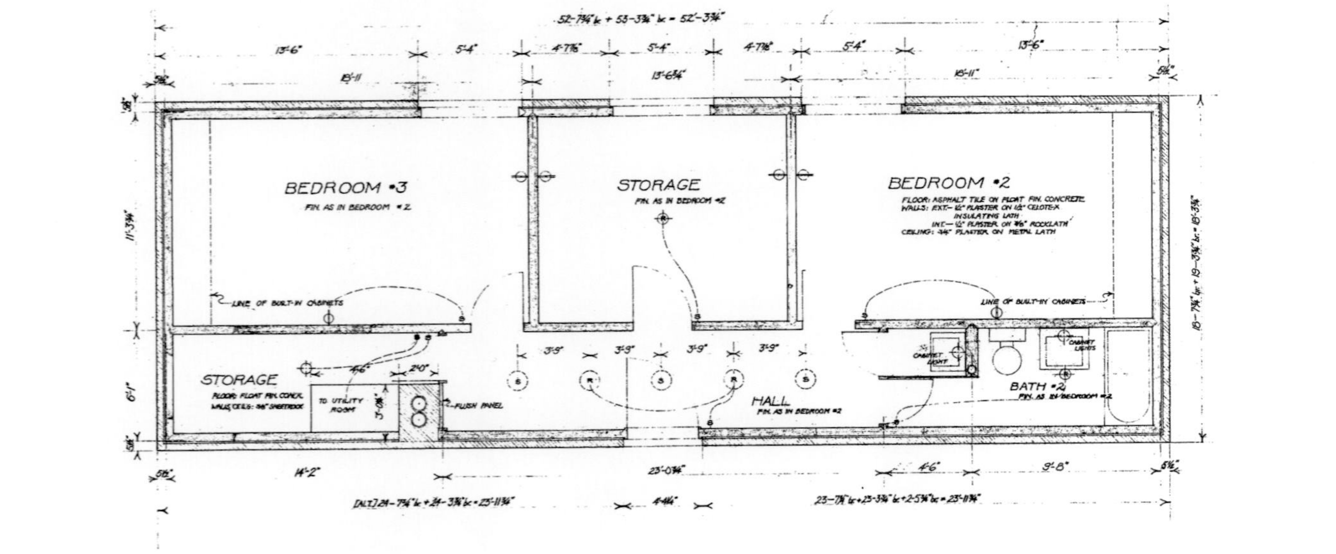

FLOOR PLAN
ALL DOORS 1¾" x HIGH FLUSH DOORS
S- INDICATES SKYLIGHT, R- RECESS FIXTURE

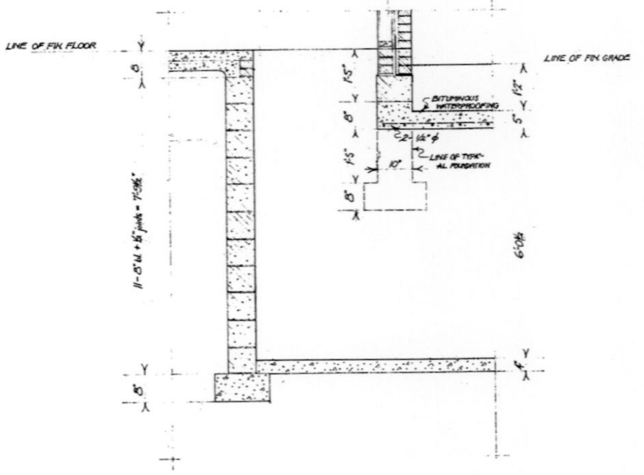

SECTION THROUGH
UTILITY ROOM HATCHWAY
SCALE ½"=1'-0"

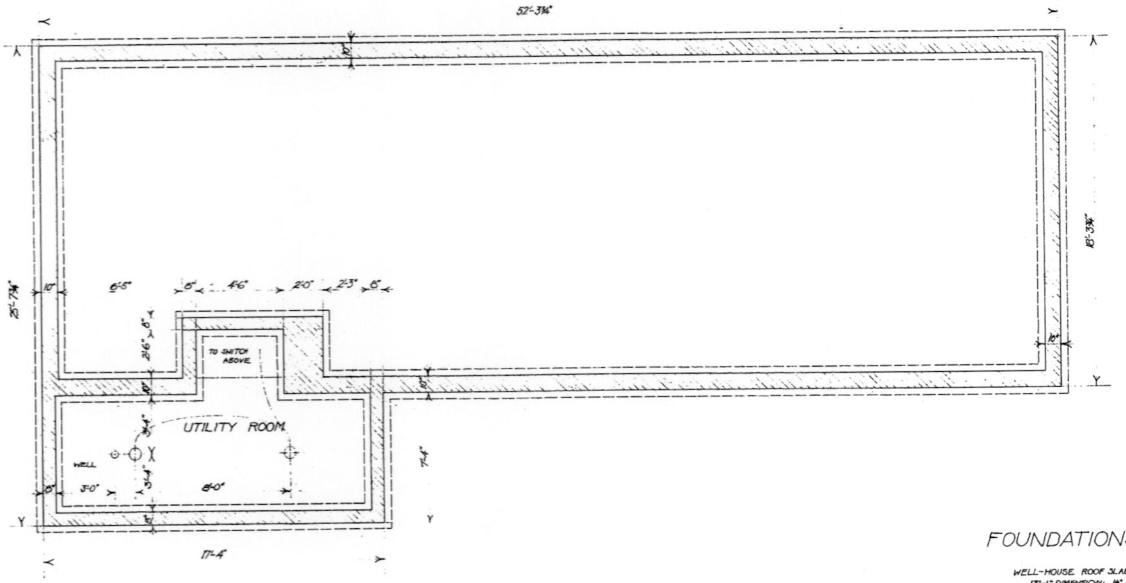

FOUNDATIONS
WELL-HOUSE ROOF SLAB REINFORCING:
13'-1" DIMENSION: ½" ϕ 1'-0" o.c.
7'-6" DIMENSION: ½" ϕ 8" o.c.

Philip Johnson, Brick House, final plans and section, 1948.

Philip Johnson, Glass House, final plans, 1948.

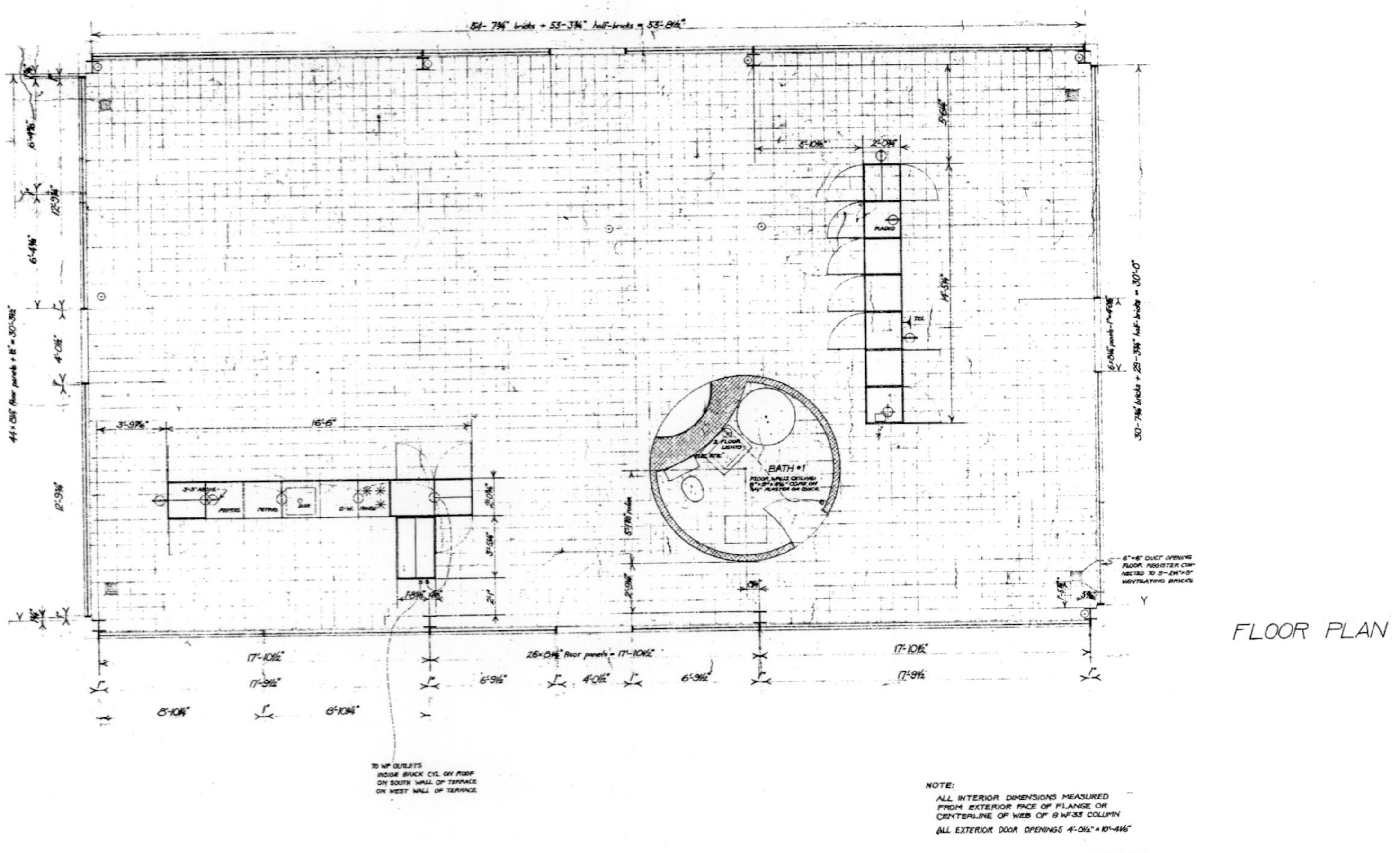
FLOOR PLAN
BATH #1
NOTE:
ALL INTERIOR DIMENSIONS MEASURED FROM EXTERIOR FACE OF FLANGE OR CENTERLINE OF W2B OF 8 WF 33 COLUMN
ALL EXTERIOR DOOR OPENINGS 4'-0½" × 10'-4⅛"

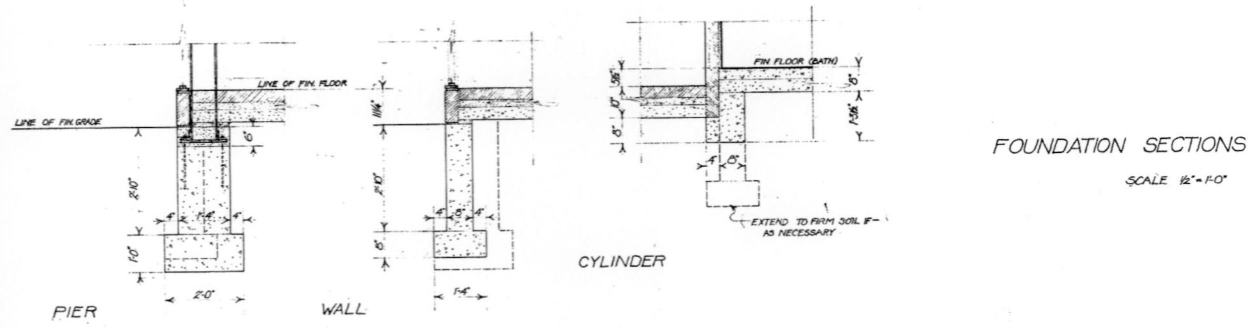
FOUNDATION SECTIONS
SCALE ½" = 1'-0"
LINE OF FIN. GRADE
LINE OF FIN. FLOOR
FIN. FLOOR (BATH)
EXTEND TO FIRM SOIL IF AS NECESSARY
PIER
WALL
CYLINDER

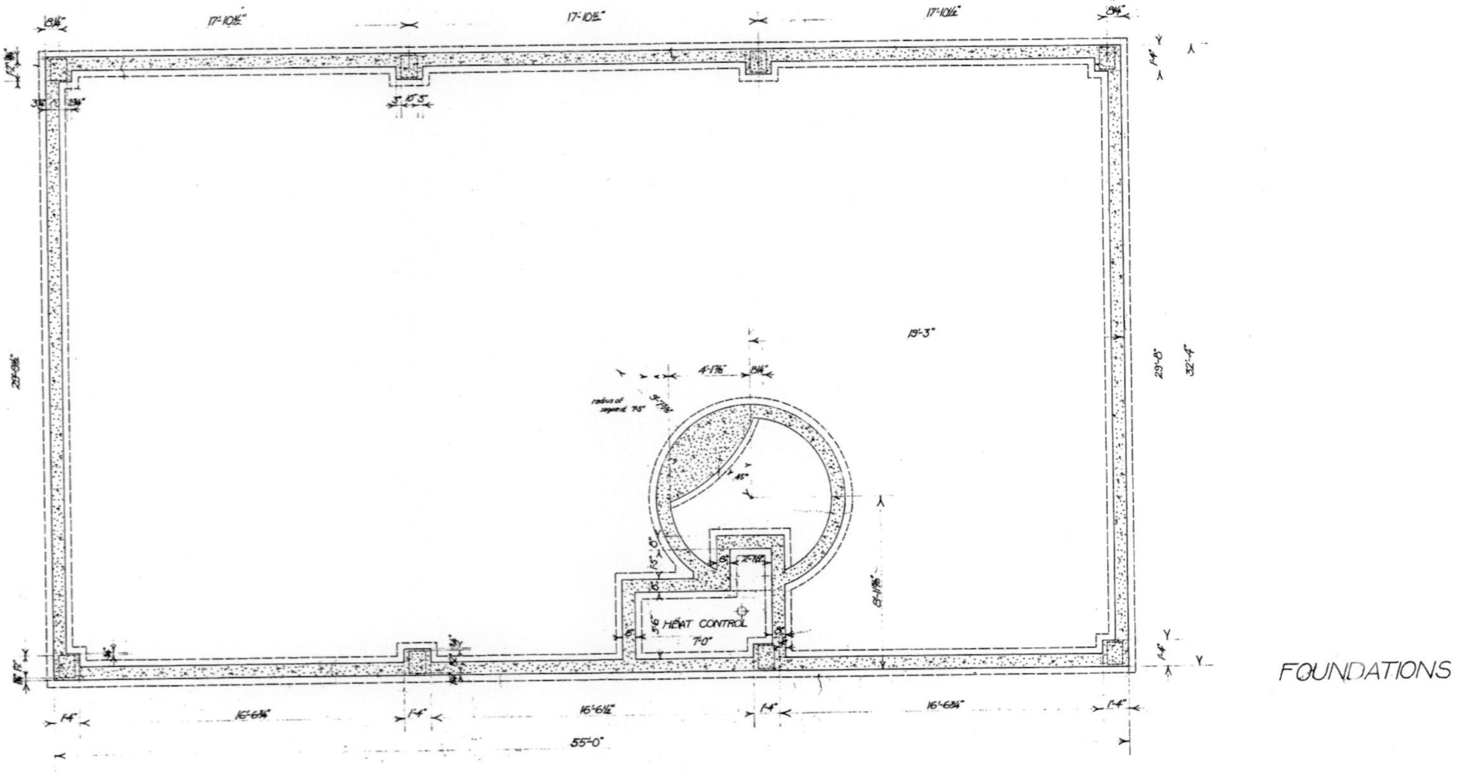
FOUNDATIONS
HEAT CONTROL
55'-0"

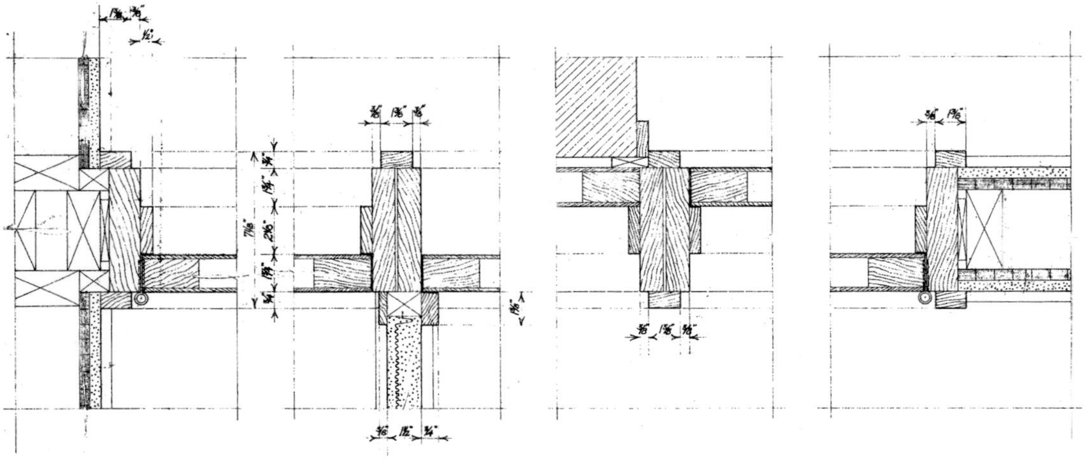

JAMB
AT 90° WALL; HEAD SIMILAR

MULLION
SOUTH HALL END

MULLION
NORTH HALL END

TYPICAL JAMB

INTERIOR TRIM
BRICK HOUSE

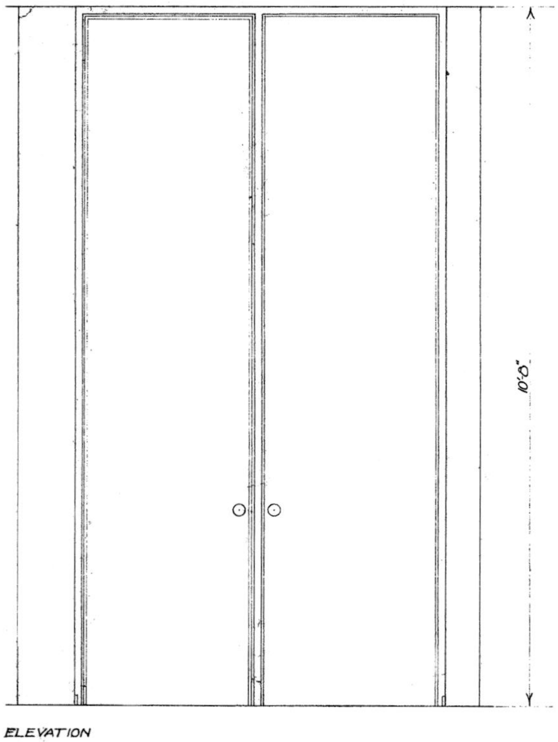

ELEVATION

SOUTH HALL END
NORTH SIMILAR 3/4" = 1'-0"

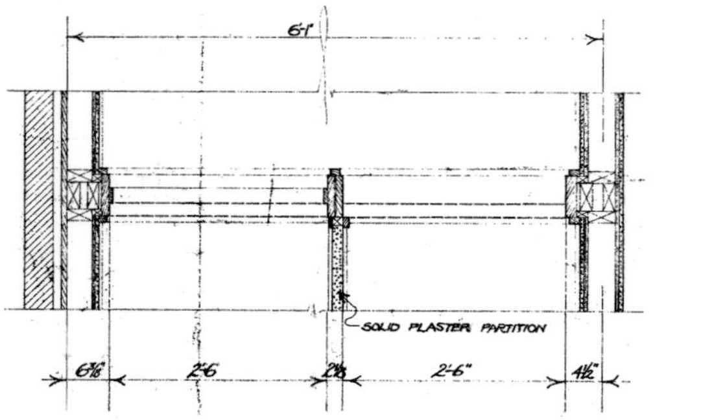

PLAN

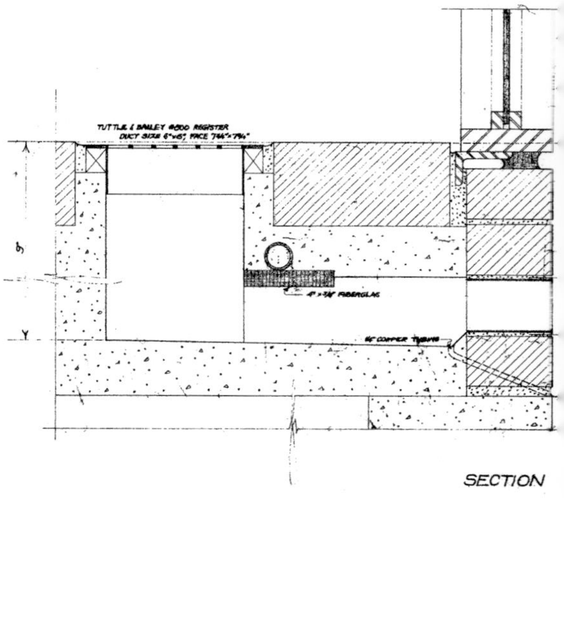

SECTION

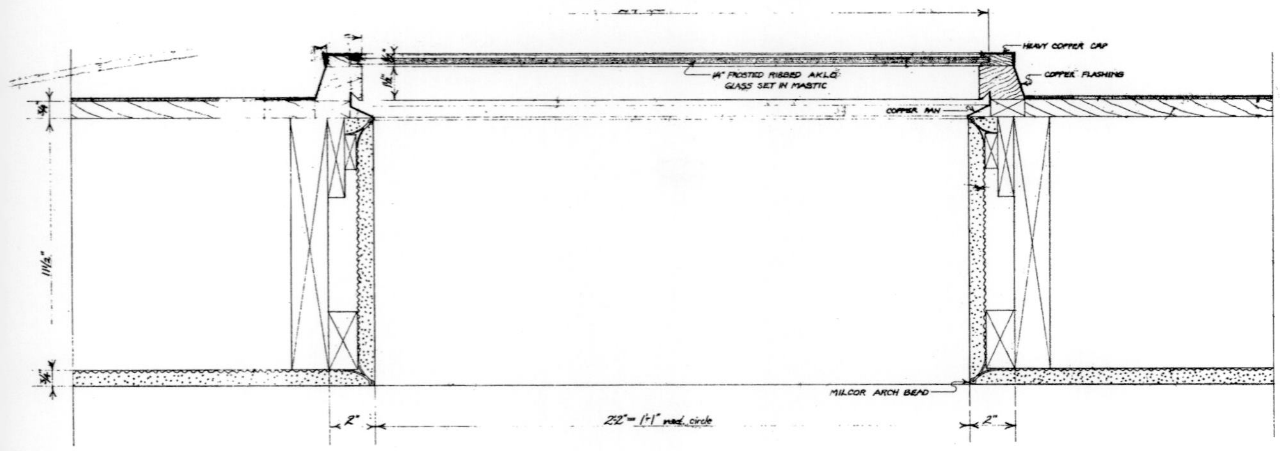

HALL SKYLIGHTS
BRICK HOUSE

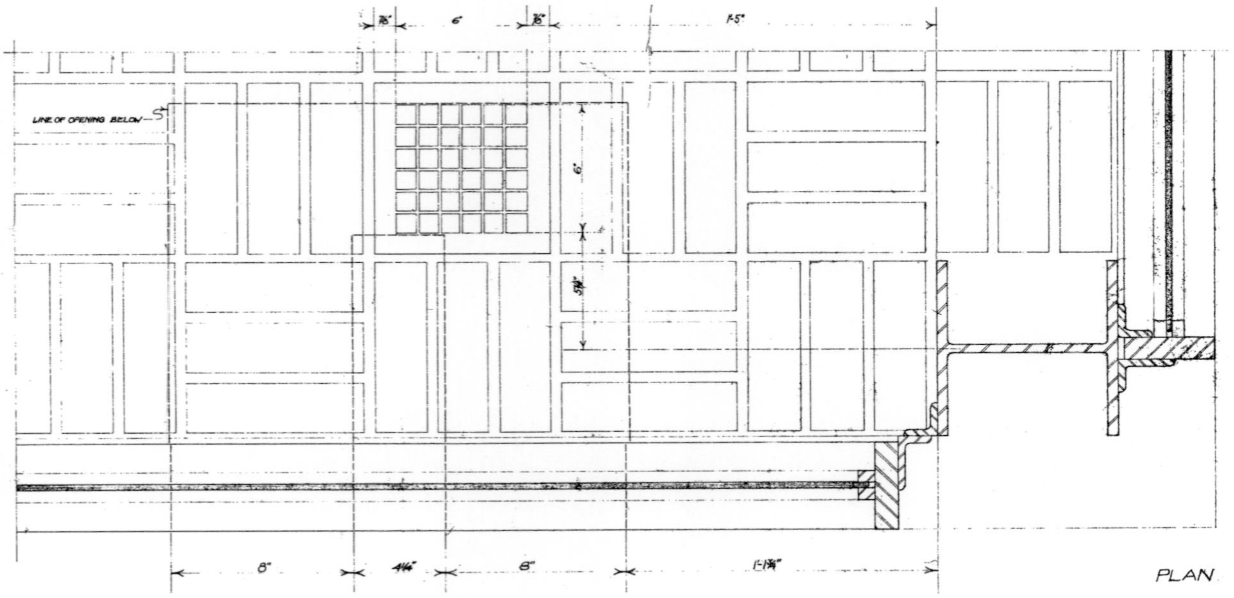

FLOOR VENTILATORS
GLASS HOUSE

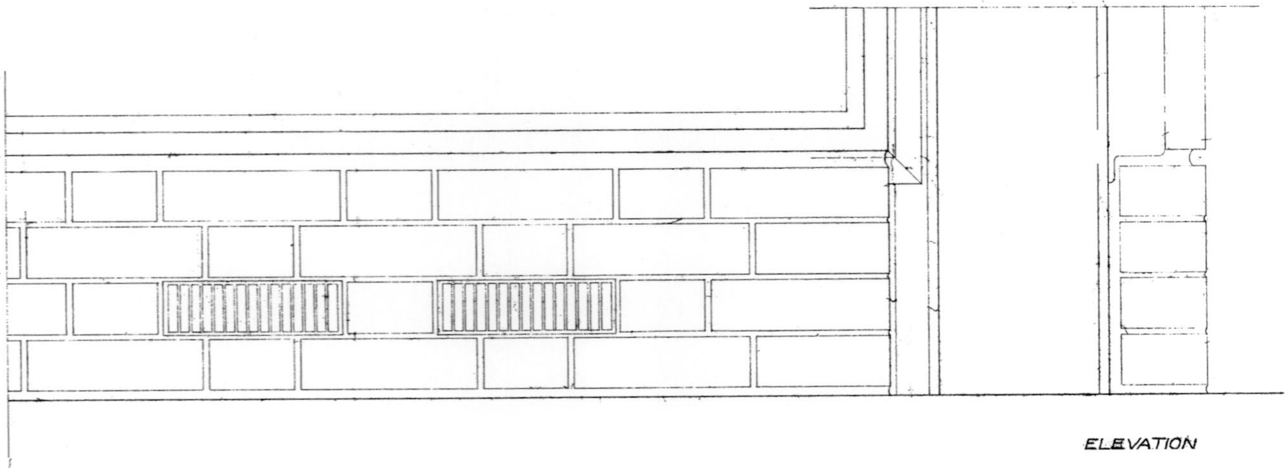

Philip Johnson, Glass House and Brick House, miscellaneous details, 1948.

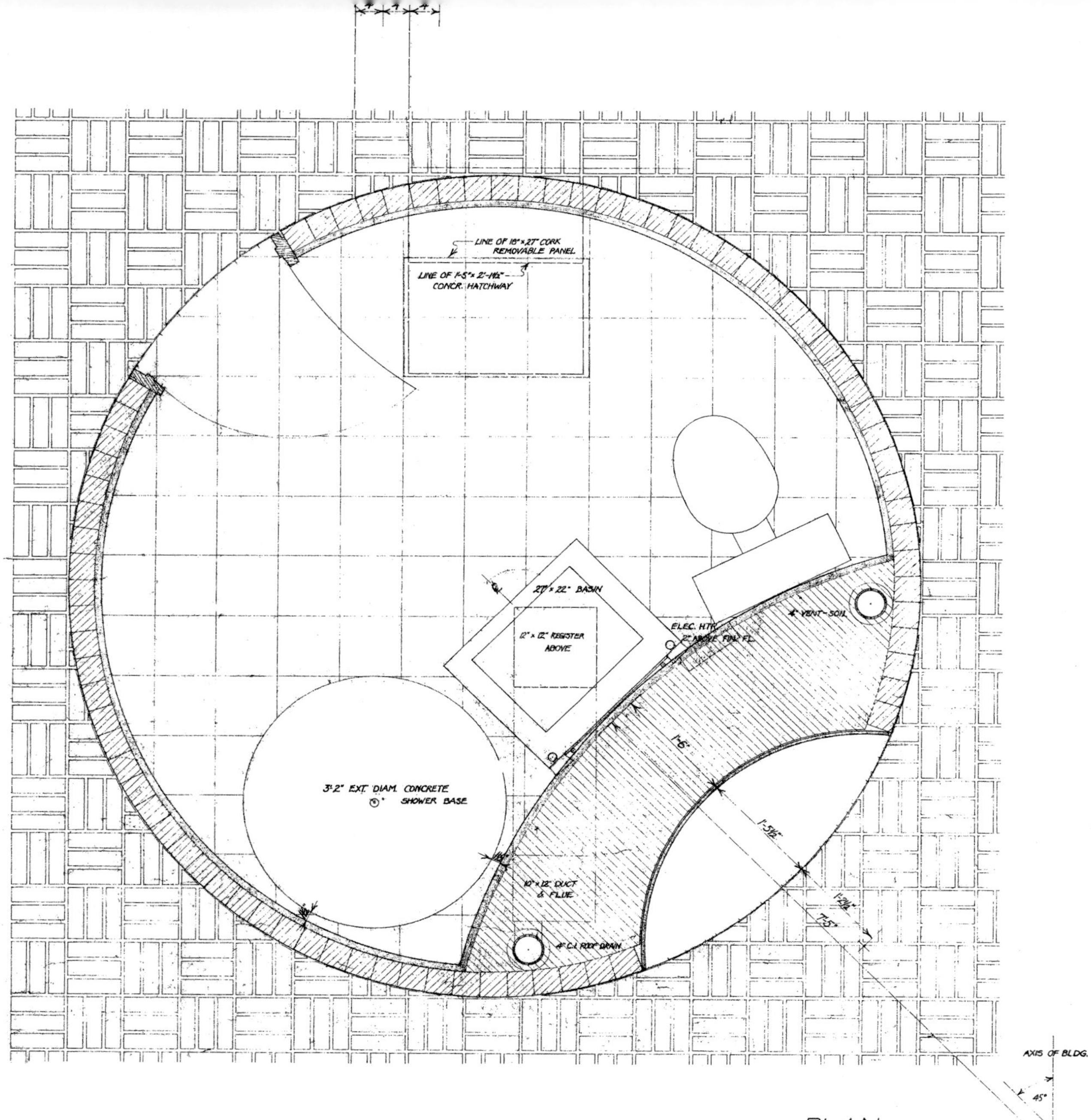

PLAN

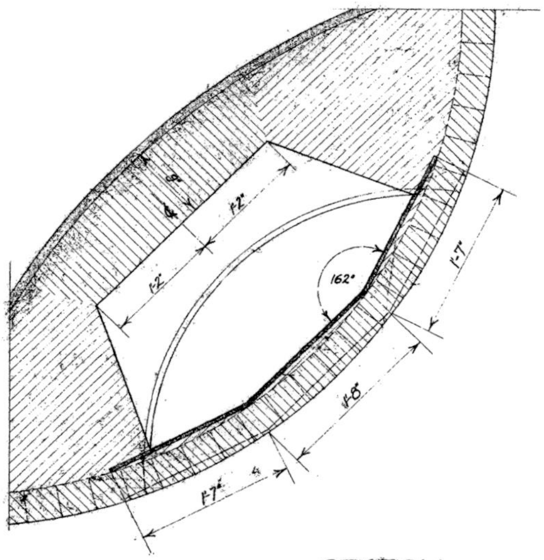

SECTION
AT THROAT

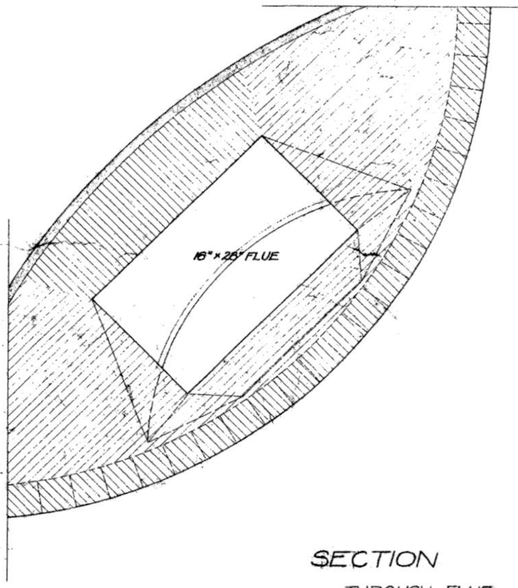

SECTION
THROUGH FLUE

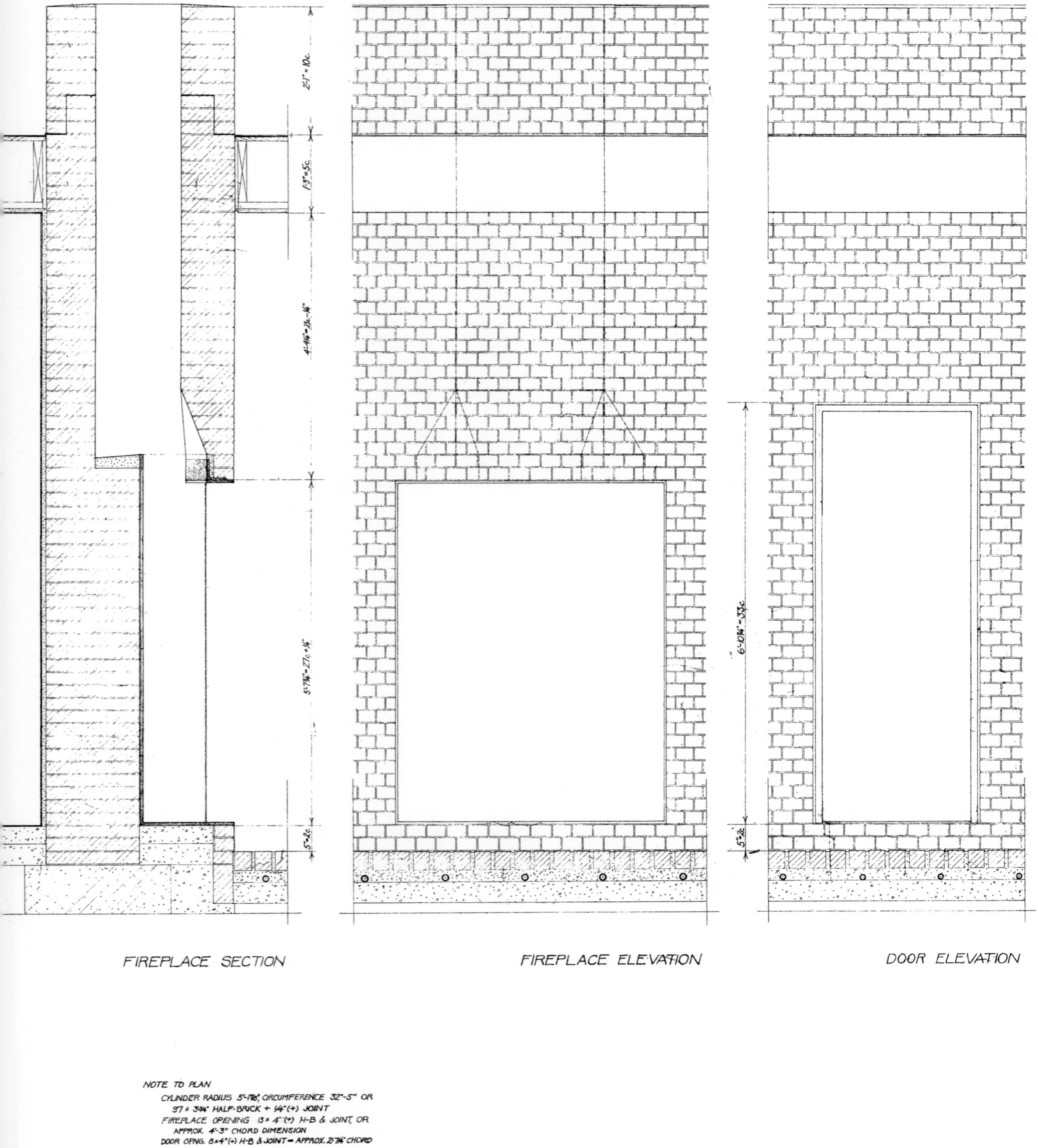

Philip Johnson, Glass House, detail of brick cylinder, 1948.

STRUCTURAL
BEAM & COLUMN
CONNECTIONS

SECTION THROUGH BEAM & CHANNEL WEBS

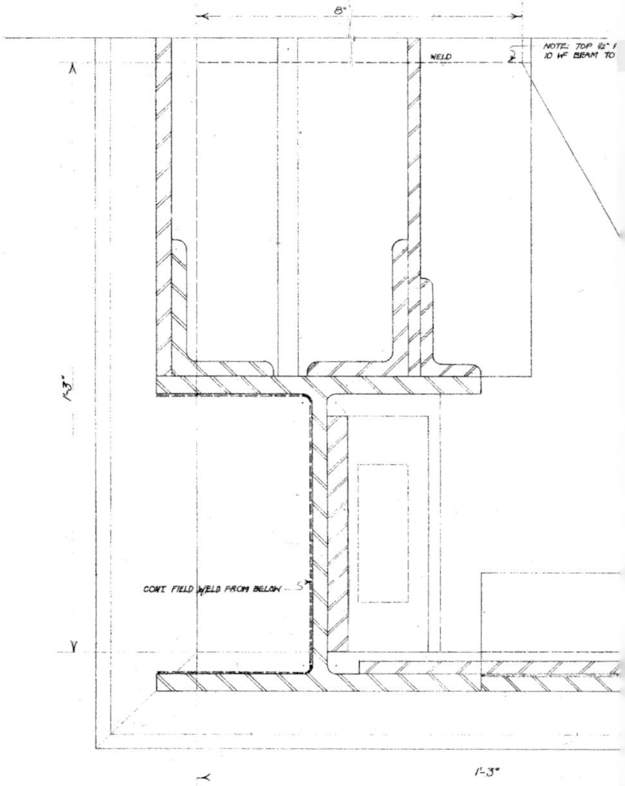

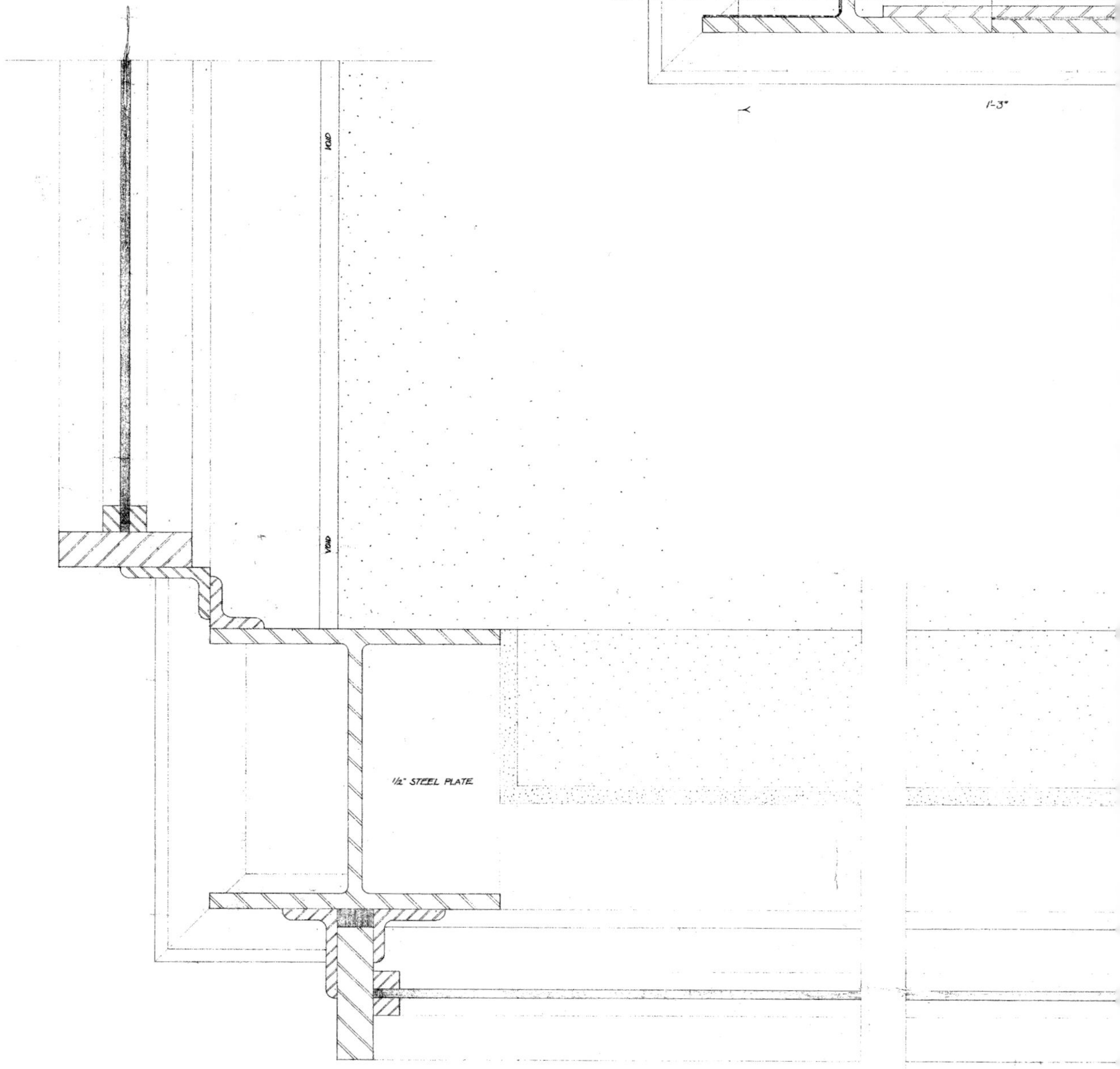

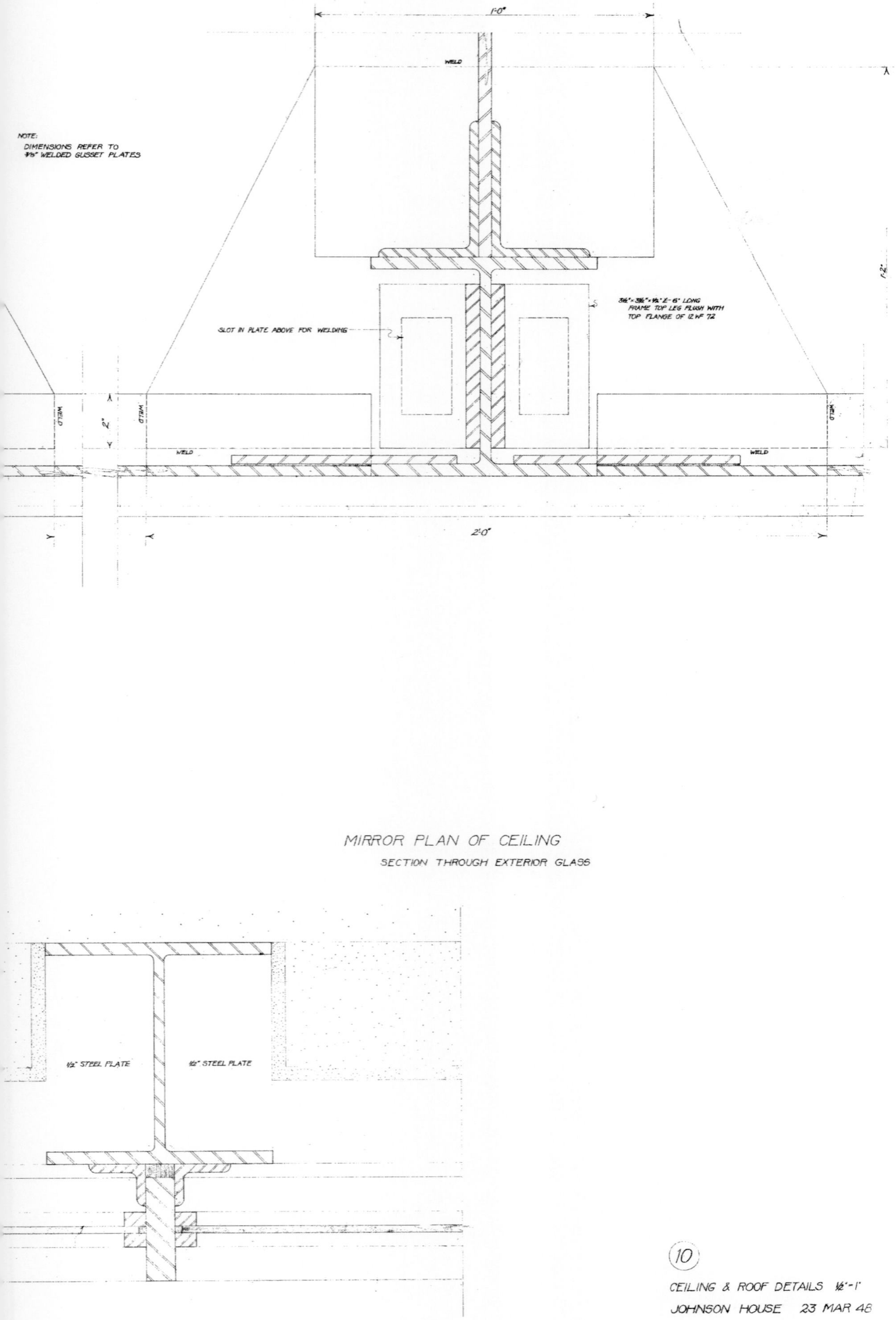

Philip Johnson, Glass House, detail of ceiling and roof, 1948.

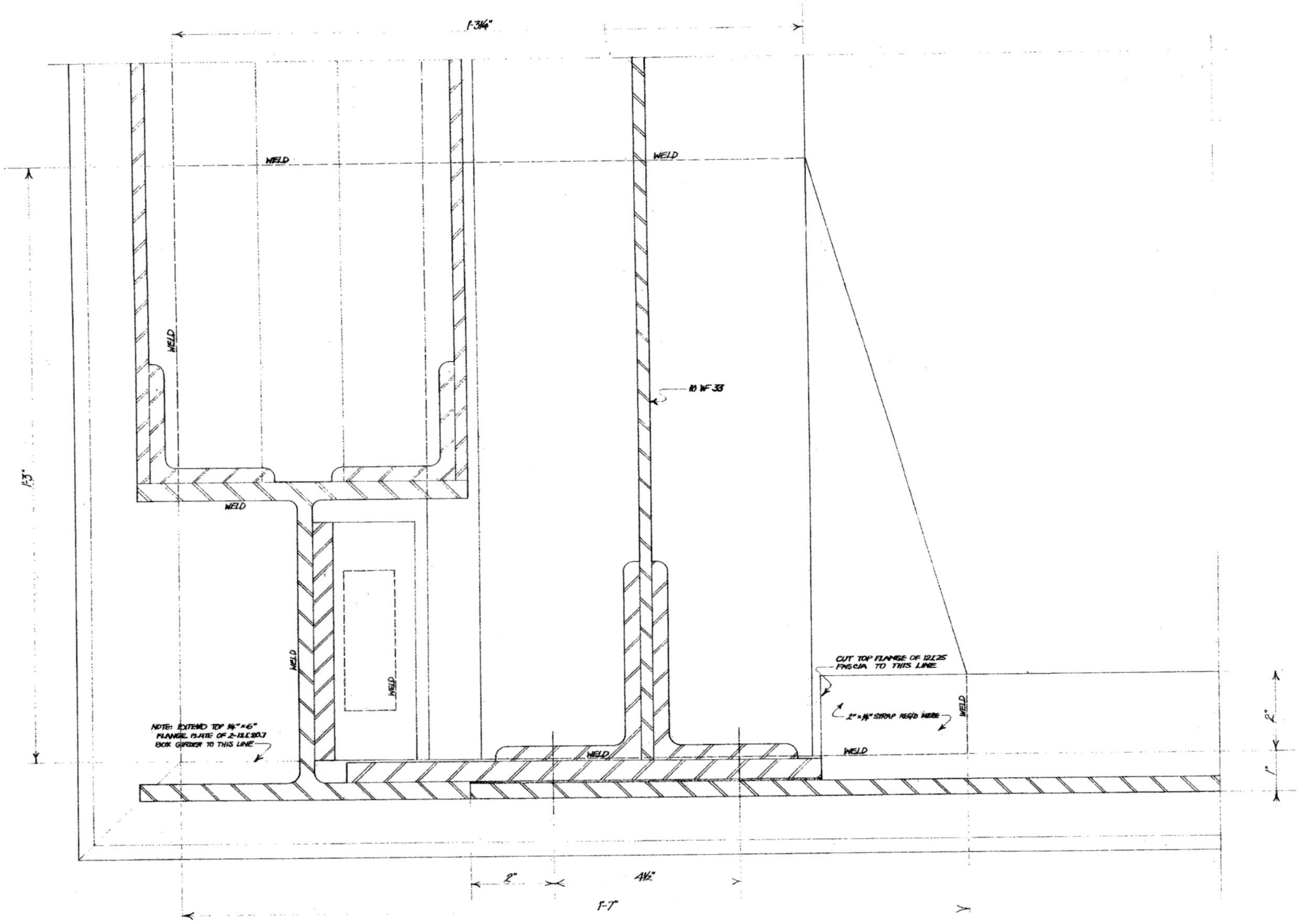

Philip Johnson, Glass House, detail of corner connection, 1948.

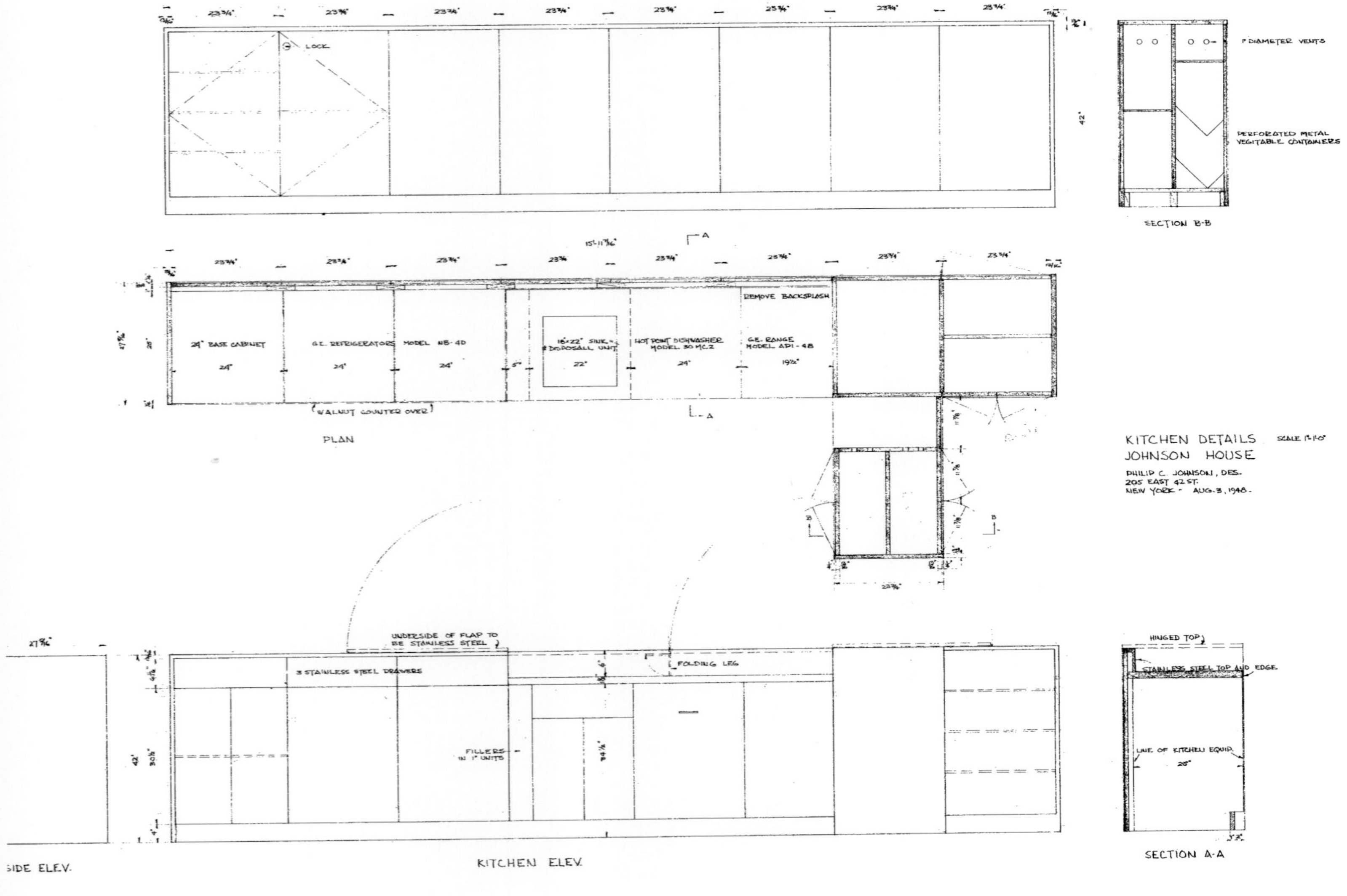

Philip Johnson, Glass House, detail of kitchen, 1948.

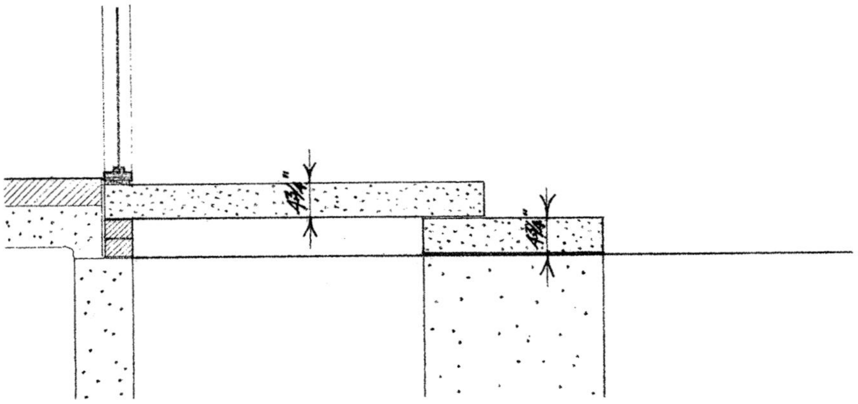

SECTION

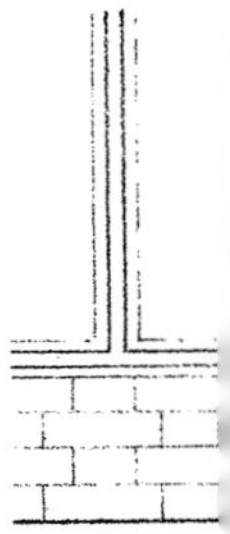

GLA

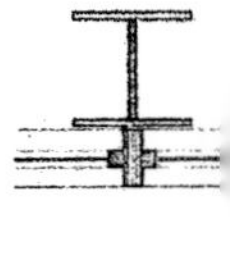

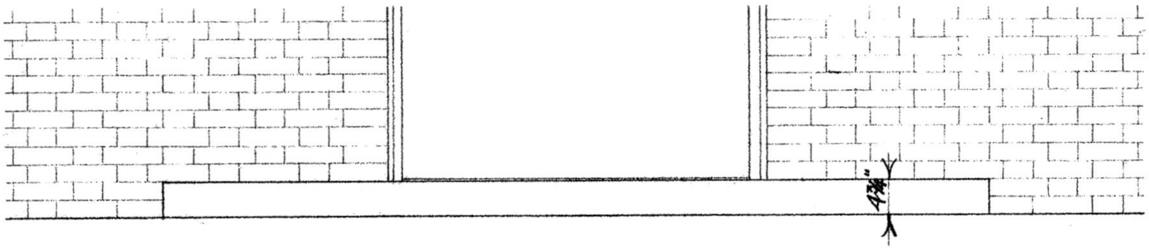

ELEVATION

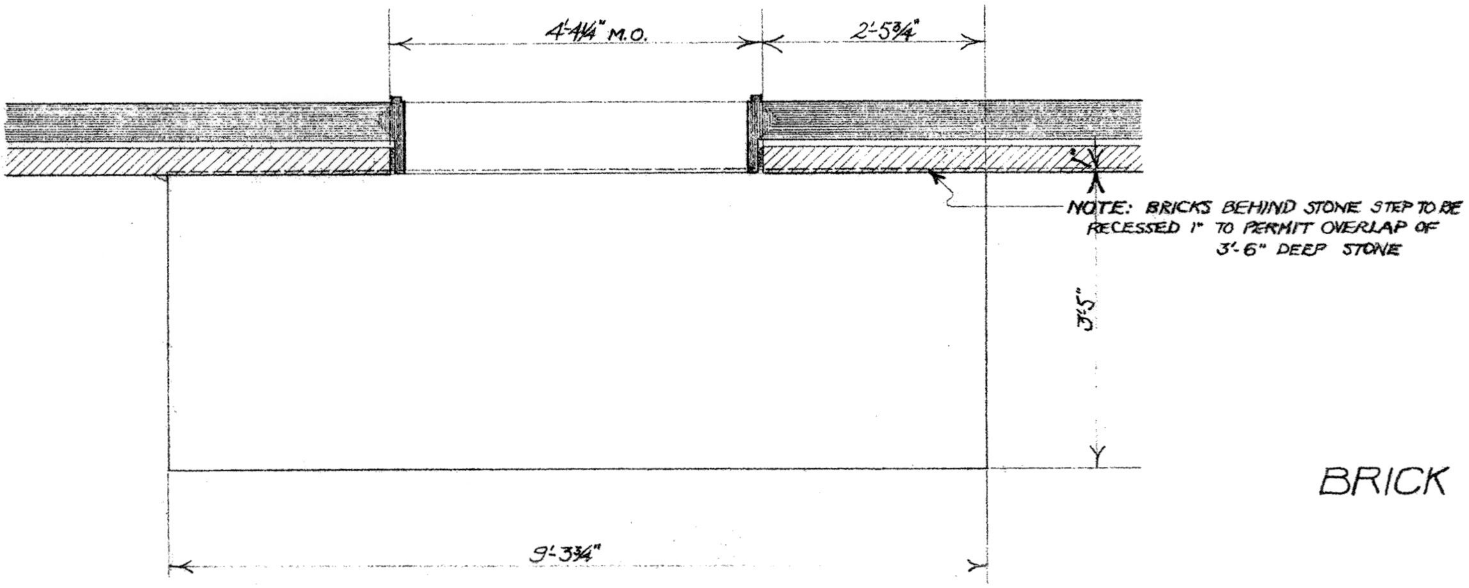

BRICK H

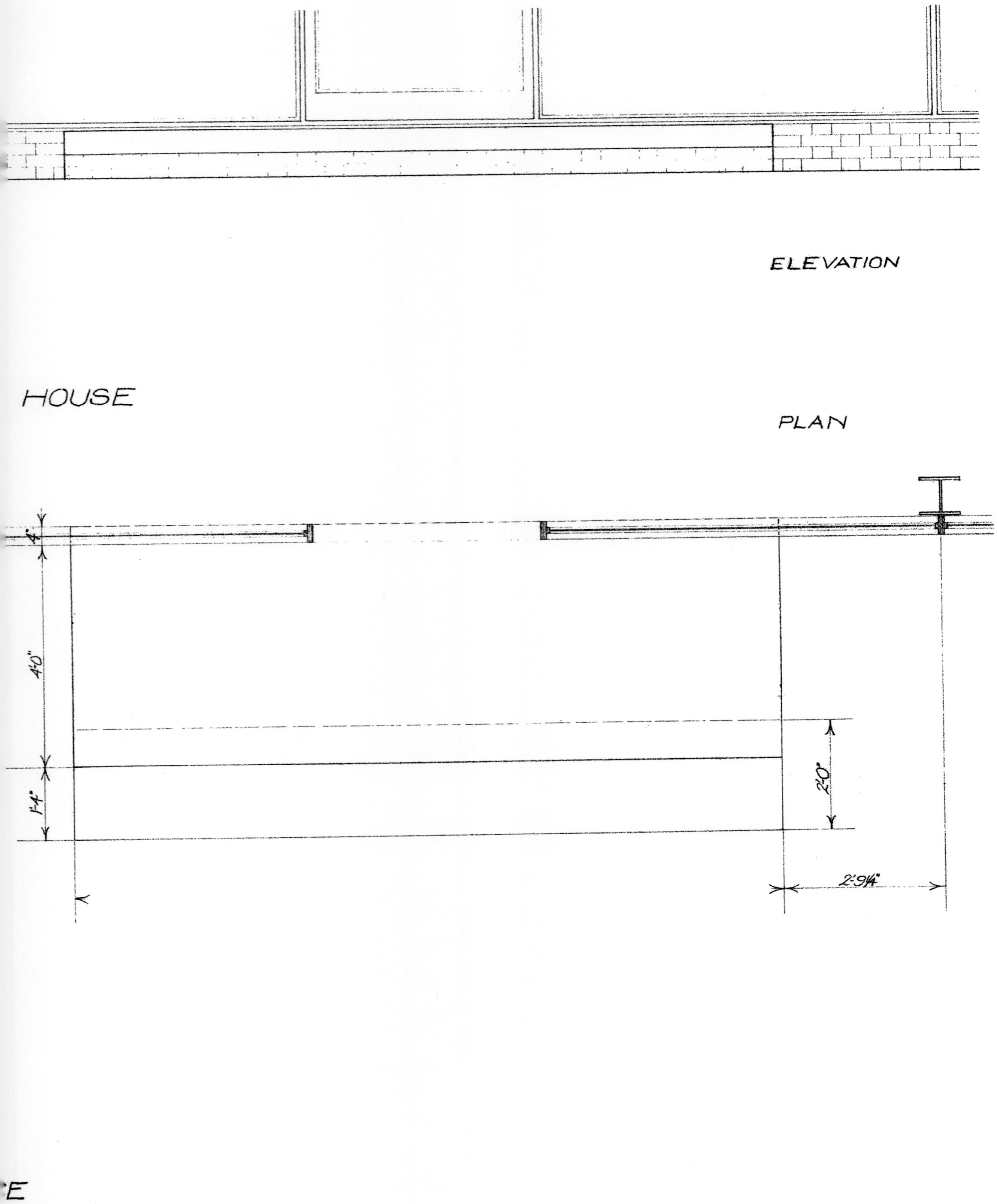

Philip Johnson, detail of stone entrance steps for the Glass House and the Brick House, 1948.

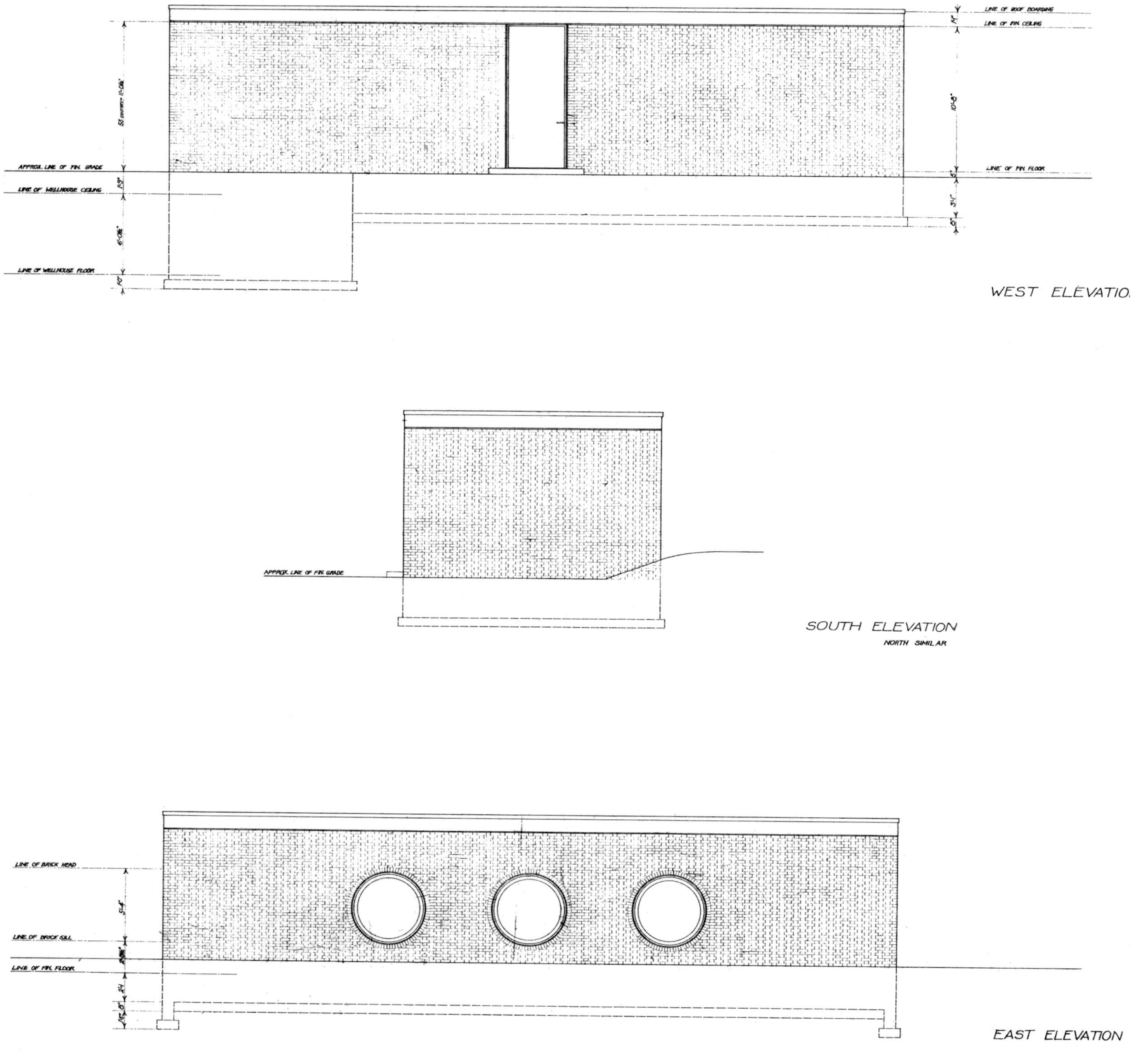

Philip Johnson, Brick House, final elevations, 1948.

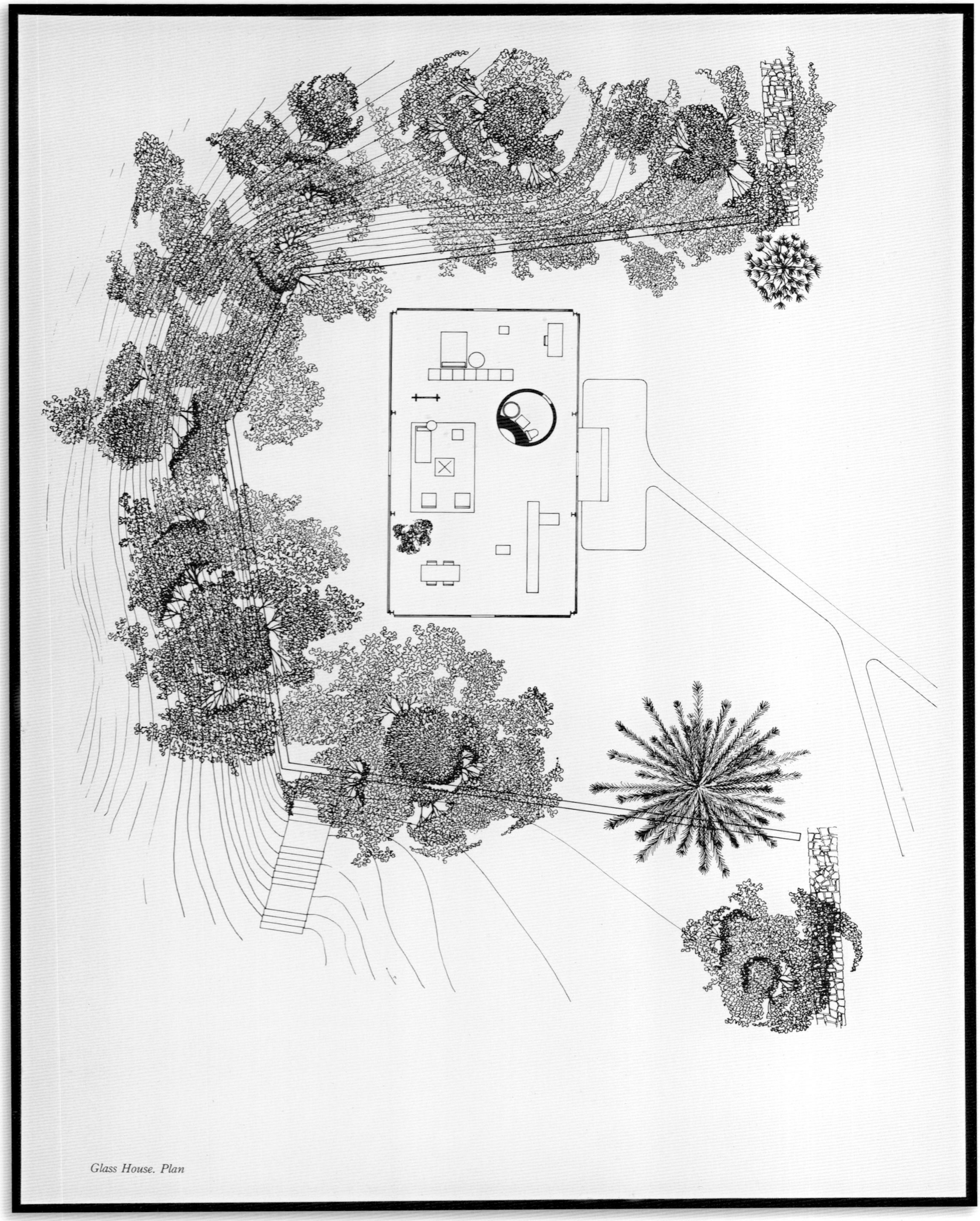

Philip Johnson, Glass House, final site plan.
Courtesy of Philip Johnson Papers, Getty Research Institute, Los Angeles.

INDEX

All photographs of the artworks are courtesy of Sotheby's, unless otherwise noted.

ARCHITECTS

60 **KRIER Léon**
A Future for the Glass House in New Canaan, 2010
Ink on Canson paper
12 3/4" x 9 3/4"
Courtesy of the architect

64 **KRUECK Ronald A.**
Untitled, 2010
Mixed media
24" x 1 1/2" x 24"
Courtesy of the architect

88 **KUWABARA Bruce**
A Sketch for a Country House, Southern Ontario, 2006
China marker on tracing paper
24" x 12"
Courtesy of the architect

41 **LIBESKIND Daniel**
Mies van der Rohe Memorial, 1987–2010
Drawing on print
26 1/2" x 1 1/4" x 25 1/2"
Courtesy of the architect

104 **LOHAN Dirk**
The Prodigies of Modernism, 2010
Architectural model
Courtesy of the architect

80 **LYNN Greg**
BlobWall © brick, 2008
Panelite plastic
36" x 30" x 18"
Courtesy of the architect

72 **MAYNE Thom**
San Francisco Federal Building, layered building skin detail
Printed on Hawk Mountain Condor Natural Paper by Jack Duganne
28 1/4" x 25 1/4"
Photograph by Nic Lehoux
Courtesy of the architect

67 **MCKENNA Marianne**
Torys LLP Offices, 2010
Two sketches and photo collage
24" x 18" (largest)
Photographs © Maris Mezulis/Test Corporation (left) and © Tom Arban/Tom Arban Photography (right). Courtesy of the architect

81 **MEIER Richard**
Getty Center, Getty 1 – Research Institute, spring 1998
Lithograph
28" x 20 1/2"
Edition 5/20
Courtesy of the architect

70 **MORI Toshiko**
Ribbon of Time and Space, 2010
Work on paper
11 1/4" x 1/4" x 17"
Courtesy of the architect

78 **MOSS Eric Owen**
If Not Now, When?, 2010
Model
11" x 11" x 11"
Courtesy of the architect

76 **MOSTAFAVI Mohsen**
Untitled, 2010
Two drawings
13 3/4" x 3" x 13 3/4" each
Courtesy of the architect

83 **PATKAU Patricia and John**
Peterson/Munck House, Quadra Island, British Columbia, 2010
Printed drawing
11" x 17"
Courtesy of the architects

89 **PELLI Cesar**
Arsht Performing Arts Center of Miami, 1998
Lithograph
20" x 14"
Courtesy of the architect

75 **PERRAULT Dominique**
Bibliothèque nationale de France, Paris, 1990
Drawing, 16 1/2" x 11 3/4"
Courtesy of the architect

84 **PRIX Wolf D.**
Central Los Angeles Area High School #9 for the Visual and Performing Arts, 2010
Architectural model
15" x 10" x 16 1/4"
© COOP HIMMELB(L)AU Wolf D. Prix / W. Dreibholz & Partner ZT GmbH
Courtesy of the architect

101 **RADZINER Ron**
Untitled, 2010
Pastel
25 3/4" x 19 1/2"
Courtesy of the architect

54 **RASHID Hani**
B-scapes, 2004
Iris print
24" x 13 1/4"
Courtesy of Asymptote Architecture

87 **ROBERTSON Jaquelin T.**
Two in One, 2010 (detail)
Four photographs in a double-sided frame
8 1/2" x 1 1/2" x 10 1/2"
Photographs by Robert Walker (top) and James Vaughn/National Trust for Historic Preservation (bottom)
Courtesy of the architect

71 **ROCHE Kevin**
The Farnsworth House Meets the Johnson House, 2010
Paper cut print
20 1/4" x 16 1/4"
Courtesy of the architect

102 **ROGERS Richard**
Wimbledon House, Wimbledon, England, 1968–69
Drawing
16 1/2" x 11 3/4"
© Rogers Stirk Harbour & Partners
Courtesy of the architect

95 **SAUCIER Gilles**
Found Object / Objet Trouvé, Helsinki, 2003 (printed 2010)
Archival pigmented ink on Hahnemuhle Photo Rag
46 3/4" x 35"
Courtesy of the architect

61 **SCARPA Lawrence**
Untitled, 2010
Drawing
9" x 12"
Courtesy of the architect

74 **SELLDORF Annabelle**
Pika House, 2007
Photograph
8" x 10"
Courtesy of the architect

43 **SHIM Brigitte and Howard SUTCLIFFE**
The Integral House, 2009
Model/mixed media
60" x 1/2" x 40"
Courtesy of the architects

92 **SIZA Álvaro**
Untitled, 2010
Mixed media
20" x 1" x 20"
Courtesy of the architect

93 **SMITH Adrian**
Blaze a Trail, 3/16/2010
Painting on paper
30" x 22 1/2"
Courtesy of the architect

91 **TANGE Kenzo** (1913–2005)
Fuji Television Headquarters Building, Tokyo, Japan, 1996
Lithograph
20" x 16"
Courtesy of Mrs. Kenzo Tange, Paul Noritaka Tange, and Tange Associates, Tokyo

98 **TIGERMAN Stanley**
Untitled, 1983
Drawing
27 1/2" x 19 1/2"
Courtesy of the architect

100 **TSAO Calvin**
Turning a Corner, January 2010
Giclée print on watercolor paper
11" x 18"
Courtesy of the architect

86 **TSCHUMI Bernard**
Glass Video Gallery, Gröningen, The Netherlands, 1990
Digital print on board
31" x 31"
© Pinkster und Tahl
Courtesy of the architect

58 **VINCI John**
Johnson and *Mies*, 2010
Two drawings
30" x 50" each
Courtesy of the architect

42 **VIÑOLY Rafael**
Untitled, April 2010
Charcoal drawing on paper
18" x 12"
Courtesy of the architect

96 **WILLIAMS Tod and Billie TSIEN**
North View, March 2010
Mounted photograph
20" x 12 1/2"
Courtesy of the architects
Photograph courtesy of Shegning Zhang

85 **WOODS Lebbeus**
Mountain Building, 1981
Lithographic crayon on mylar on backing paper
20" x 30"
Courtesy of the architect

89 **ZARDINI Mirko and Lukas MEYER**
Urban Bus No. 2, 1995
Digital print
19 1/2" x 19 3/4"
Courtesy of the architects

LANDSCAPE ARCHITECTS

113 BALMORI Diana
Experiment #3, 2009
Work on paper
30" x 1/4" x 22.5"
Edition 1/5
Courtesy of the designer

114 GEUZE Adriaan
Botanic Bridge Gwangju, 2001
Two prints
32" x 1/4" x 34" each
Courtesy of the designer

116 GUSTAFSON Kathryn and Amyn NASSER
Morbras Meeting Point #1, 2010
Dye Sub on 0.042-inch aluminum
30" x 45"
Edition 1/3 (+ AP, +PP)
© Amyn Nasser
Courtesy of the designer and photographer

106 HILDERBRAND Gary
Almost Nothing, 2010
Photo collage
9 3/4" x 11"
Courtesy of the designer
Photographs courtesy of Paul Warchol and Eirik Johnson

108 HOOD Walter J.
Madama #1, 2010
Inkjet print/collage
11" x 1/4" x 15 1/2"
Courtesy of the designer and Magnolia Press, Oakland

112 LATZ Peter
Duisburg Nord Landschaftspark, Duisburg, Germany, 1990–2002, 2010
Three mounted photographs:
Piazza Metallica (Michael Latz)
Cowper Square (Peter Schäfer)
Garden in former ore bunker (Michael Latz)
12" x 1/4" x 12" each
Courtesy of the designer

110 SMITH Ken
Grass Glass, 2010
Lenticular print
16" x 16"
Courtesy of the designer

ARTISTS

140 CELMINS Vija
Starfield, 2010
Mezzotint
26 3/8" x 35 7/8"
AP 1/10
Courtesy of the artist

134 DAVIS Lynn
Maison de Verre, France, 2001
Digital print
20" x 20"
Edition 3/10
Courtesy of Lynn Davis Studio

136 DIAO David
Perfect Arrangement at 1/4 Scale, 2005
Laser-cut felt
36" x 42 1/2"
Edition of 5
Courtesy of the artist
Photograph courtesy of S. Baker

127 HAEG Fritz
Edith + Ludwig and Philip + David, 2010
Two embroidered pillowcases
28" x 18 1/2" each
Courtesy of the artist

131 KALMAN Maira
People who live in glass houses…, 2005
Inkjet print
11" x 15 3/4"
Edition 18/36
Courtesy of the artist and Julie Saul Gallery, New York

125 LAWLER Louise
Red, Yellow, Blue, Black and White and Light, 1984/2007
Black-and-white photograph
4 11/16" x 4"
AP 6/20 (Edition of 100)
Courtesy of the artist and Metro Pictures, New York

118 LEIBOVITZ Annie
Phillip Johnson, the Glass House, New Canaan, Connecticut, 2000
Archival pigment print
20" x 24"
Courtesy of the artist

122 **MANGLANO-OVALLE Iñigo**
Gravity Is a Force to Be Reckoned With (Untitled Repose), 2010
Giclée print on paper
12" x 30"
Edition 1/10
Courtesy of the artist

137 **MORRIS Robert**
Untitled (Nine Fiberglass Sleeves), 1967
Drawing
30" x 21 3/4"
© 2010 Robert Morris / Artists Rights Society (ARS), New York
Courtesy of the artist

124 **NOGAI Juergen and Julius SHULMAN** (1910–2009)
Glass House Commissions, 2007
Color print
20" x 16"
Courtesy of the artists and the Philip Johnson Glass House

120 **OLDENBURG Claes and Coosje VAN BRUGGEN** (1942–2009)
The Architect's Handkerchief, 1997
Screenprint and collé
31 1/4" x 23 1/2"
Courtesy of Claes Oldenburg

133 **PLENSA Jaume**
Anonymous IX, 2005
Aluminum
14 5/8" x 14 5/8" x 13 3/4"
Courtesy of the artist and Richard Gray Gallery, Chicago

129 **PRICE Ken**
Zwig, 2009
Fired and painted clay
7 3/4" x 15" x 11"
Courtesy of the artist and Matthew Marks Gallery, New York

143 **ROSENQUIST James**
Sketch for Tosca III, 2010
Collage, with mixed media
9 3/4" x 11"
Courtesy of the artist

145 **RUSCHA Ed**
Busted Glass #32, 2009
Acrylic on museum board paper
11 1/4" x 14 1/4"
© Ed Ruscha
Courtesy of the artist and Gagosian Gallery, New York

130 **SALLE David**
Untitled, 2008
Oil on lithograph
22" x 30"
© David Salle/Licensed by VAGA, New York
Courtesy of the artist and Mary Boone Gallery, New York

144 **STELLA Frank**
Der Angriff, 1971
Gray and black silk screen
18" x 24"
Edition of 150
© 2010 Frank Stella/Artists Rights Society (ARS), New York

141 **TAYLOR Al** (1948–1999)
Sideffects of Danish Doorway, 1996
Pencil and conté crayon on paper
16 1/4" x 12 3/4"
Courtesy of Debbie Taylor
© The Estate of Al Taylor

128 **TWOMBLY Alessandro**
Untitled (Figures of Eros), 2008
Acrylic and oil crayon on paper
30 1/2" x 22 3/4"
Courtesy of the artist and Fred Torres Collaborations, New York

138 **WELLING James**
0962, 2006
Inkjet print
40" x 58 1/2"
Courtesy of David Zwirner, New York

126 **WOODS Richard**
Wood Stack, 2009
Painted wood sculpture
44" x 18" x 14"
Courtesy of the artist and Perry Rubenstein Gallery, New York

DESIGNERS

156 2 x 4
Ecstasy, 2010
Animation
© 2 x 4, 2010
Courtesy of the designers

153 BAAS Maarten
Where There's Smoke
Gerrit T. Rietveld's 1934 Zig-Zag Chair
29 1/2" x 15" x 16 1/2"
Created for Moss New York
Courtesy of the designer

165 BELLINI Mario
Design for Motorway Service Areas, Lainate, Italy, 1989–2010
Architectural model in Plexiglas case, framed print, and DVD
28" x 19 1/4" x 11 1/2"
Courtesy of Mario Bellini Architects

154 BONETTI Mattia
Table Garden, 2010
Terra-cotta architectural model
18" x 12 1/2" x 4 1/2"
Courtesy of the designer

150 BOUROULLEC Ronan and Erwan
Untitled, 2010
Drawing (recto and verso)
13 3/4" x 1/4" x 9 3/4"
Courtesy of the designers

158 BOYM Constantin
A Souvenir of Modernism, 2010
Mixed media
8" x 8" x 8"
Courtesy of the designer

162 GAMPER Martino
sedia db, 2009
Drawing
16" x 11 3/4"
Courtesy of the designer

164 HICKS Sheila
Diagonal II Tipped, 2005
Textile
16 1/4" x 18" x 1"
Courtesy of the designer

160 KAGAN Vladimir
A Fantasy Visit with Philip Johnson in the Glass House, 2010
Three drawings
14" x 16" each
Courtesy of the designer

148 PESCE Gaetano
Organic Building, 1993
Drawing
12" x 15 1/2"
Courtesy of the designer

149 RASHID Karim
Dekon 2, 2006
Glass table
58" x 26" x 14 1/2"
Courtesy of the designer

167 REPUCCI Demian
Philip vs. Mies (Four Seasons), 2010
Digital chromogenic print
27" x 19"
Signed AP 2/5 (Edition of 100)
Courtesy of the designer

163 RISOM Jens
Glass House Commissions, 2007
Four stools
23" x 23" x 19 1/2" each
Courtesy of the designer and the Philip Johnson Glass House, New Canaan

146 SCHER Paula
Modernism USA, 2010
Silk screen
34 1/2" x 23 1/2"
Courtesy of the designer

152 STUDIO MAKKINK & BEY
Studioscape, 2010
Print on textile and embroidery
39 1/2" x 39 1/4"
Edition 1/1
Courtesy of the designers

ACKNOWLEDGMENTS

This publication was born from an idea proposed and led by Christy MacLear, executive director of the Philip Johnson Glass House, and Whitney French, executive director of Farnsworth House. The Philip Johnson Glass House and Assouline Publishing would like to acknowledge the board of trustees and the executive staff of the National Trust for Historic Preservation for their support of this project and the Glass House Center for Modernism board of advisors: Johan Eveland, Paul Goldberger, Edwin B. Hathaway, Robert Rubin, William Ruprecht, and Robert A. M. Stern. In addition, we would like to thank the MODERN VIEWS project leadership, including John Bryan, Amalia Dayan and Adam Lindemann, Paul Goldberger, Richard Gray, Phyllis Lambert, Tobias Meyer and Mark Fletcher, and Cindy Pritzker.

The Philip Johnson Glass House would like to thank editorial director Esther Kremer, editor Sarah P. Hanson, designers Camille Dubois and Cecilia Maurin, photo editor Naomi Leibowitz, and production director Gina Amorelli. Moreover, we would like to thank MODERN VIEWS project director Susan Sayre Batton for shaping and editing this publication. We especially thank the following individuals and organizations that contributed images to this book: Rosamond Bernier; David Dunlap; the Getty Research Institute, Los Angeles; and, at the Museum of Modern Art, New York, in the Department of Architecture and Design, Barry Bergdoll, Philip Johnson Chief Curator of Architecture and Design, and Paul Galloway, cataloguer.

This project could not have been realized without our generous sponsor Sotheby's, especially William Ruprecht, Amy Todd Middleton, Rena Neville, Helyn Goldenberg, Tobias Meyer, James Zemaitis, Michael Moore, Susan D'Inverno, Carl Capasso, Olena Whipple, and John McKnight, and photographers Robert Bean, Jerry Fetzer, Jon Lam, Michael Tropea, Patrick de Warren, and Eric Vigil.

Lastly, the publisher would like to thank Paul Goldberger and Sylvia Lavin for their insightful texts, as well as Phyllis Lambert, who was interviewed by Dorothy Dunn of the Glass House staff. Final thanks go to the Glass House MODERN VIEWS team, including Irene Shum Allen, curator and collections manager; Dorothy Dunn, director of visitor experience and fellowships; Gretchen Mueller Burke, adjunct curator; Christa Carr, press director; Meri Erickson, manager of events and projects; and Chris Roth, development coordinator.

PHOTO CREDITS

Page 8: photograph courtesy of David Dunlap. Pages 12–17: photograph courtesy of David Dunlap. Pages 20–21: Phyllis Lambert Fonds, Collection Centre Canadien d'Architecture/Canadian Centre for Architecture, Montréal, © United Press International. Pages 28–29: photograph courtesy of David Dunlap. Page 34: photographs courtesy of Rosamond Bernier. Pages 36–37: photograph courtesy of Philip Johnson Papers, Research Library, the Getty Research Institute, Los Angeles. Pages 185–208: Unless otherwise noted, all drawings courtesy of the Architectural Drawing Archive, Philip Johnson Glass House, National Trust for HIstoric Preservation.